About This Book

D1396812

Why Is This Topic Important?

Traditionally, performance feedback in organizations has come from a single source, the boss. There are problems with this approach because it provides a limited perspective. But even if receiving feedback from several sources is desirable, without the process known as 360-degree feedback, it is impractical and expensive for organizations to put into practice.

What Can You Achieve with This Book?

You can use this book to make 360-degree feedback work in your organization. It provides guidance for individuals inside organizations and for consultants working with organizations that are looking to create and maintain an effective 360-degree feedback process. It explores the use of 360-degree feedback in the leadership development process by drawing on the lessons CCL has learned through its research and practice of the 360-degree process since the mid-1970s.

How Is the Book Organized?

The book is organized into four chapters. Chapter 1 describes the purposes and uses of 360-degree feedback. It describes what 360-degree feedback is, how it works, and why it is needed in organizations and for individuals. Chapter 2 deals with implementing a 360-degree feedback process, from determining your organization's need and readiness to collecting the data. Chapter 3 discusses facilitating the feedback to individuals and groups, and Chapter 4 describes ways to enhance the success of a 360-degree feedback process. Chapter 5 closes the discussion by examining trends and future uses of the 360-degree feedback process.

Throughout the book, checklists, worksheets, and examples help readers apply the authors' guidance to their own situations. Additional resources include a glossary of 360-degree feedback terms and recommended resources for in-depth information on implementing and evaluating a 360 process.

About Pfeiffer

Pfeiffer serves the professional development and hands-on resource needs of training and human resource practitioners and gives them products to do their jobs better. We deliver proven ideas and solutions from experts in HR development and HR management, and we offer effective and customizable tools to improve workplace performance. From novice to seasoned professional, Pfeiffer is the source you can trust to make yourself and your organization more successful.

Essential Knowledge Pfeiffer produces insightful, practical, and comprehensive materials on topics that matter the most to training and HR professionals. Our Essential Knowledge resources translate the expertise of seasoned professionals into practical, how-to guidance on critical workplace issues and problems. These resources are supported by case studies, worksheets, and job aids and are frequently supplemented with CD-ROMs, websites, and other means of making the content easier to read, understand, and use.

Essential Tools Pfeiffer's Essential Tools resources save time and expense by offering proven, ready-to-use materials—including exercises, activities, games, instruments, and assessments—for use during a training or team-learning event. These resources are frequently offered in looseleaf or CD-ROM format to facilitate copying and customization of the material.

Pfeiffer also recognizes the remarkable power of new technologies in expanding the reach and effectiveness of training. While e-hype has often created whizbang solutions in search of a problem, we are dedicated to bringing convenience and enhancements to proven training solutions. All our e-tools comply with rigorous functionality standards. The most appropriate technology wrapped around essential content yields the perfect solution for today's on-the-go trainers and human resource professionals.

Pfeiffer
www.pfeiffer.com
Essential resources for training and HR professionals

ABOUT THE CENTER FOR CREATIVE LEADERSHIP

The Center for Creative Leadership (CCL) is a top-ranked, global provider of executive education that develops better leaders through its exclusive focus on leadership education and research. Founded in 1970 as a nonprofit, educational institution, CCL helps clients worldwide cultivate creative leadership—the capacity to achieve more than imagined by thinking and acting beyond boundaries—through an array of programs, products, and other services.

Ranked in the top ten in the *Financial Times* annual executive education survey, CCL is headquartered in Greensboro, North Carolina, with campuses in Colorado Springs, Colorado; San Diego, California; Brussels, Belgium; and Singapore. Supported by more than five hundred faculty members and staff, it works annually with more than twenty thousand leaders and three thousand organizations. In addition, sixteen Network Associates around the world offer selected CCL programs and assessments.

CCL draws strength from its nonprofit status and educational mission, which provide unusual flexibility in a world where quarterly profits often drive thinking and direction. It has the freedom to be objective, wary of short-term trends, and motivated foremost by its mission—hence its substantial and sustained investment in leadership research. Although CCL's work is always grounded in a strong foundation of research, it focuses on achieving a beneficial impact in the real world. Its efforts are geared to be practical and action oriented, helping leaders and their organizations more effectively achieve their goals and vision. The desire to transform learning and ideas into action provides the impetus for CCL's programs, assessments, publications, and services.

CAPABILITIES

CCL's activities encompass leadership education, knowledge generation and dissemination, and building a community centered on leadership. CCL is broadly recognized for excellence in executive education, leadership development, and innovation by sources such as *BusinessWeek, Financial Times, The New York Times,* and *The Wall Street Journal.*

OPEN-ENROLLMENT PROGRAMS

Fourteen open-enrollment courses are designed for leaders at all levels, as well as people responsible for leadership development and training at their organizations. This portfolio offers distinct choices for participants seeking a particular learning environment or type of experience. Some programs are structured specifically around small group activities, discussion, and personal reflection, while others offer hands-on opportunities through business simulations, artistic exploration, team-building exercises, and new-skills practice. Many of these programs offer private one-on-one sessions with a feedback coach.

For a complete listing of programs, visit http://www.ccl.org/programs.

CUSTOMIZED PROGRAMS

CCL develops tailored educational solutions for more than one hundred client organizations around the world each year. Through this applied practice, CCL structures and delivers programs focused on specific leadership development needs within the context of defined organizational challenges, including innovation, the merging of cultures, and the development of a broader pool of leaders. The objective is to help organizations develop, within their own cultures, the leadership capacity they need to address challenges as they emerge.

Program details are available online at http://www.ccl.org/custom.

COACHING

CCL's suite of coaching services is designed to help leaders maintain a sustained focus and generate increased momentum toward achieving their goals. These coaching alternatives vary in depth and duration and serve a variety of needs, from helping an executive sort through career and life issues to working with an organization to integrate coaching into its internal development process. Our coaching offerings, which can supplement program attendance or be customized for specific individual or team needs, are based on our ACS model of assessment, challenge, and support.

Learn more about CCL's coaching services at http://www.ccl.org/coaching.

ASSESSMENT AND DEVELOPMENT RESOURCES

CCL pioneered 360-degree feedback and believes that assessment provides a solid foundation for learning, growth, and transformation and that development truly happens when an individual recognizes the need to change. CCL offers a broad selection of assessment tools, online resources, and simulations that can help individuals, teams, and organizations increase their self-awareness, facilitate their own learning, enable their development, and enhance their effectiveness.

CCL's assessments are profiled at http://www.ccl.org/assessments.

PUBLICATIONS

The theoretical foundation for many of our programs, as well as the results of CCL's extensive and often groundbreaking research, can be found in the scores of publications issued by CCL Press and through the Center's alliance with Jossey-Bass, a Wiley imprint. Among these are landmark works, such as *Breaking the Glass Ceiling* and *The Lessons of Experience,* as well as quick-read guidebooks focused on core aspects of leadership. CCL publications provide insights and practical advice to help individuals become more effective leaders, develop leadership training within organizations, address issues of change and diversity, and build the systems and strategies that advance leadership collectively at the institutional level.

A complete listing of CCL publications is available at http://www.ccl.org/publications.

LEADERSHIP COMMUNITY

To ensure that the Center's work remains focused, relevant, and important to the individuals and organizations it serves, CCL maintains a host of networks, councils, and learning and virtual communities that bring together alumni, donors, faculty, practicing leaders, and thought leaders from around the globe. CCL also forges relationships and alliances with individuals, organizations, and associations that share its values and mission. The energy, insights, and support from these relationships help shape and sustain CCL's educational and research practices and provide its clients with an added measure of motivation and inspiration as they continue their lifelong commitment to leadership and learning.

To learn more, visit http://www.ccl.org/community.

RESEARCH

CCL's portfolio of programs, products, and services is built on a solid foundation of behavioral science research. The role of research at CCL is to advance the understanding of leadership and to transform learning into practical tools for participants and clients. CCL's research is the hub of a cycle that transforms knowledge into applications and applications into knowledge, thereby illuminating the way organizations think about and enact leadership and leader development.

Find out more about current research initiatives at http://www.ccl.org/research.

For additional information about CCL, please visit http://www.ccl.org or call Client Services at (336) 545–2810.

Leveraging the Impact of 360-Degree Feedback

John Fleenor
Sylvester Taylor
Craig Chappelow

Pfeiffer
A Wiley Imprint
www.pfeiffer.com

Published by Pfeiffer
A Wiley Imprint
989 Market Street, San Francisco, CA 94103-1741 www.pfeiffer.com

For additional copies/bulk purchases of this book in the U.S. please contact 800-274-4434.

Pfeiffer books and products are available through most bookstores. To contact Pfeiffer directly call our Customer Care Department within the U.S. at 800-274-4434, outside the U.S. at 317-572-3985, fax 317-572-4002, or visit www.pfeiffer.com.

Pfeiffer also publishes its books in a variety of electronic formats. Some content that appears in print may not be available in electronic books.

Library of Congress Cataloging-in-Publication Data:

Fleenor, John W.
 Leveraging the impact of 360-degree feedback / John Fleenor, Sylvester Taylor, Craig Chappelow.
  p. cm.
 Includes bibliographical references and index.
 ISBN 978-0-470-18409-7 (pbk.)
  1. 360-degree feedback (Rating of employees) 2. Employees—Rating of. 3. Organizational effectiveness. 4. Leadership. I. Taylor, Sylvester. II. Chappelow, Craig. III. Title.
 HF5549.5.R3F5527 2008
 658.3'125—dc22
                      2007050460

Acquiring Editor:	Lisa Shannon	Editor:	Rebecca Taff
Director of Development:	Kathleen Dolan Davies	Assistant Editor:	Marisa Kelley
Marketing Manager:	Brian Grimm	Manufacturing Supervisor:	Becky Morgan
Production Editor:	Michael Kay		

10 9 8 7 6 5 4 3 2

CONTENTS

ACKNOWLEDGMENTS

The authors would like to recognize Dave Bracken and Carol Timmreck for their input during the development of this book. They also recognize Pete Scisco, their editor at CCL; Karen Lewis; and Joanne Ferguson for their assistance in publishing this work.

INTRODUCTION

O ne of the most significant trends in the leadership development field over the past twenty years has been the growth of 360-degree feedback (Chappelow, 2004). It has been called one of the most notable management innovations in recent times (Atwater & Waldman, 1998).

There are numerous books, guides, and other publications that describe in detail various aspects of 360-degree feedback. Many of these publications, several of which are referenced in this book, focus on particular aspects of this method and have allowed practitioners to increase their understanding of this sometimes complex process. As one of its original architects, the Center for Creative Leadership (CCL) has made significant contributions to the literature on 360-degree feedback.

This publication presents CCL's view on how to successfully implement a 360-degree feedback process. There are other effective methods, but for the purposes of this book, we will focus on how to optimize 360-degree feedback when used for developmental purposes. The recommendations in this book provide guidance based on our experience and the experience of our clients.

Given the popularity of 360-degree feedback, research is generally lagging behind practice. Over the years, there has not been a lot of research that focuses on the complex process of implementing 360-degree feedback (Brutus, Fleenor, & London, 1998). In this book, we cite research to support our conclusions in areas in which relevant research has been conducted; however, there are a number of areas of 360-degree feedback that have not been extensively researched. In these cases, we will provide what we believe are best practices based on CCL's experiences.

This book is written for the HR professional in an organization or independent consultant who is considering implementing or expanding the use of 360-degree feedback and integrating it into the organization's leadership development efforts. To help HR professionals successfully implement the 360-degree feedback process in their organizations, this book reveals what CCL has learned over the past thirty years about 360-degree feedback. For example:

- 360-degree feedback should not be implemented as a stand-alone event. In addition to the assessment, there must be a development planning and follow-up component.
- Boss support is critical for the 360 process, as well as for getting participants to set specific development goals.
- The 360-degree feedback process works best if it begins with the top executives of the organization then cascades through the organization.
- A shoddy administration of a 360-degree feedback process can be fatal to future administrations.
- The timing of the 360 process should take into account the organizational realities that could dilute or confound its impact.

THE DIFFERENCE IS DEVELOPMENTAL

In its simplest terms, feedback in the context of an organization refers to the information a person receives from co-workers related to his or her work behavior. In addition to day-to-day interpersonal communication, the traditional medium for periodic feedback is performance appraisal. Appraisal carries the weight of setting goals and tracking two aspects of performance: the development of competence and the achievement of results. For these and other reasons, employees tolerate these formal performance evaluations. However, managers and employees often express their dislike of performance appraisals and say they don't do a very good job of developing skills or guaranteeing results (London, 1997).

Traditionally, performance feedback in organizations has come from a single source, the boss. There are problems with this approach to collecting performance information. For example, assessment from a single source, such as a boss, provides a limited perspective. It is also subject to bias, which affects the quality and the accuracy of the feedback (London & Beatty, 1993). In the case of managers assessing direct reports, bosses often do not have the time or the opportunity to observe their employees in all possible situations. Employees may behave one way with their bosses and a different way with their peers.

Another type of feedback is peer feedback, in which coworkers at the same level in an organization provide input on an individual's performance. Again, this approach provides data from only one perspective and may result in biased and inaccurate feedback. Peers often find themselves in competitive situations with their cohorts and may be reluctant to provide overly positive feedback. Some peers may believe that they will look better by providing negative feedback about their coworkers.

Peers, direct reports, and customers often have more detailed information than bosses alone about how employees do their jobs. Further, coworkers usually care deeply about performance issues, because when others don't do their jobs well, it affects their work as well as the productivity of the organization as a whole.

In this book, we refer to the person being assessed as the *participant.* The participant selects a number of coworkers (called *raters*) to participate in the feedback process. The definitions of these and other important terms can be found in the glossary in Appendix B.

Receiving feedback from several sources may be desirable, but without the process known as 360-degree feedback, it is impractical and expensive. Most professional and managerial employees have experienced 360-degree feedback in some form, either by receiving ratings from their boss, peers, and direct reports, or by rating others. Church (2000) estimates that almost 30 percent of U.S. companies use some form of 360-degree feedback, while Brutus and Derayeh (2002) report that 43 percent of Canadian companies surveyed use 360-degree feedback.

Since 2000, CCL has administered one of its 360 instruments, Benchmarks, in more than fifty countries. Based on the number of participants receiving feedback, the top ten countries (excluding the United States) are

1. Canada

2. The United Kingdom

3. Singapore

4. Australia

5. Germany

6. France

7. The Netherlands

8. Belgium

9. New Zealand

10. Switzerland.

In 2001, CCL surveyed 395 U.S. organizations that purchase management and leadership development services (Bradley, 2001). Included in the survey were 212 CCL clients and 183 non-client organizations. The survey results related to usage of 360-degree feedback indicate the following:

- The majority of respondents (63 percent) stated that their organizations used 360-degree feedback.

- CCL clients used 360-degree feedback slightly more than non-client organizations (75 percent versus 61 percent).

- All of the industry segments surveyed said they were using 360-degree assessments to some extent.

- Pharmaceuticals and government agencies were most likely to use 360-degree feedback, while nonprofit organizations were least likely.

By using a 360-degree feedback process, it becomes relatively straightforward to focus on specific behaviors and collect ratings and comments from a wide range of raters. Because of its structure, thoroughness, and anonymity, 360-degree feedback is likely to be accepted by the individuals receiving the feedback (Atwater, Brett, & Charles, 2007). In addition, organizations can use the feedback chiefly for developmental purposes, which potentially results in more positive outcomes than traditional performance appraisals.

HOW TO USE THIS BOOK

The guidance in this book on the use of 360-degree feedback in the leadership development process draws on the lessons learned through research and practice at CCL that began in the mid-1970s. Since that time, CCL has partnered with hundreds of clients to deploy 360-degree feedback processes in their organizations, both large and small, in North America and around the world.

First and foremost, you can use this book to make 360-degree feedback work in your organization. It contains step-by-step suggestions for successful implementation and a collection of best practices that CCL has observed and tested over the years. Much of the guidance is based on research insights that provide a solid foundation on how 360-degree feedback works, and that research is cited throughout the book so that you can broaden your understanding of this essential development tool.

For a comprehensive review of the professional literature on 360-degree feedback, you can consult any of several books dedicated to that topic. Four recommended titles are *Maximizing the Value of 360-Degree Feedback* (Tornow, London, & CCL Associates, 1998), *The Art and Science of 360-Degree Feedback* (Lepsinger & Lucia, 1997), *The Power of 360-Degree Feedback* (Waldman & Atwater, 1998), and *The Handbook of Multisource Feedback* (Bracken, Timmreck, & Church, 2001). The References and Recommended Resources listed at the end of the book contain leads to more in-depth treatment of various issues in the field.

HOW THIS BOOK IS ORGANIZED

The book is organized into five chapters. Chapter 1 describes the purposes and uses of 360-degree feedback, how it works, why it is needed, and the importance of multiple perspectives and the role of 360-degree feedback in developing leaders for organizational roles. Chapter 2 deals with implementing a 360-degree feedback process, including clarifying the need, checking to see that your organization is ready, the differences between standardized and customized instruments, how to prepare participants and raters, and how to collect the data.

Chapter 3 describes how to facilitate the feedback, and deals with such issues as setting the context, working in one-on-one sessions, and dealing with issues of self and rater agreement. Chapter 4 describes ways to enhance the success of a 360-degree feedback process, which includes such topics as development plans, getting the boss's support, best practices, and evaluation. Finally, in Chapter 5, we sketch trends and future directions in the field of 360-degree feedback initiatives.

Throughout the book we include worksheets, checklists, and other tools to use or adapt in planning and implementing a 360-degree process in your organization. In addition to a reference list of the sources we accessed during the writing of this book, we include a list of additional sources that provide a broader, deeper examination of 360-degree initiatives and issues.

The Purpose and Uses of 360-Degree Feedback

Most employees want to do a good job; however, many are unaware of the impact that their behavior has on their effectiveness on the job. Feedback can help employees identify what they are doing well and build on those skills, correct problems, and develop new skills that improve the organizations in which they work.

Feedback is usually defined as information provided to an employee related to the behavior of that person on the job or the results of that behavior. It is usually intended to strengthen desired behaviors or to suggest changes in undesired behaviors. Feedback can be a powerful stimulus for change, under the following conditions:

- The feedback tells the person that something important is not as it should be.
- The person is able to focus his or her energy constructively.
- The person has the resources to turn this energy into action.

Almost all of us want to know how well we are doing our jobs. In fact, when we do not receive feedback, we often seek it on our own by asking others (bosses, coworkers, friends) to provide feedback on our performance. Receiving feedback is an important motivational factor that can lead to increased satisfaction. Feedback is important because it can enhance self-awareness by highlighting strengths and can facilitate growth by pointing out areas in need of development. We learn from the outcomes of our behavior, and feedback is an important factor in helping us improve our performance.

Further, the impact of 360-degree feedback can be significant when it is embedded in a larger leadership development process. Research shows that 360-degree feedback can improve performance and lead to behavior change over time (Atwater, Waldman, Atwater, & Cartier, 2000; Smither, London, & Reilly, 2005; Walker & Smither, 1999).

Despite its potential to bring about positive behavioral changes and to develop leadership across organizations, feedback remains a rare commodity in day-to-day organizational life. This is because people generally don't like to provide feedback to others, especially if it is negative. Managers often consider conducting performance reviews, often the only feedback some employees receive about their work, as one of the most difficult and unpleasant aspects of their jobs.

THE QUALITIES OF 360-DEGREE FEEDBACK

The 360-degree feedback method began as a development tool for managers. In the late 1970s, organizations began using standardized methods to collect behavioral feedback. Ann Morrison, Morgan McCall, and David DeVries published a report in 1978 that reviewed twenty-four survey instruments in use at that time and offered advice about the strengths and weaknesses of each instrument, and that report has been periodically updated (Van Velsor & Leslie, 1991; Leslie & Fleenor, 1998). By the late 1980s, the term *360-degree feedback* began to be linked with these procedures. Van Velsor and Leslie refer to multi-rater assessment as 360-degree feedback in *Feedback to Managers, Volume II* (1991).

The first attempt to integrate existing knowledge about this process was provided in 1993 by a special issue of *Human Resource Management* edited by Walter Tornow, who was then CCL's vice president of research. Since that time, the field has grown rapidly (Hedge, Borman, & Berkland, 2001). The process is also growing internationally. It is currently used extensively in North and South America, Europe, and Australia, and it is beginning to gain acceptance in Asian countries.

In the 360-degree process, feedback is solicited not only from an individual's boss and peers but also from the individual himself or herself, direct reports, superiors (the boss's peers), and others, such as customers (Testa, 2002). This is why the method became known as 360-degree feedback—it covers the entire 360 degrees of the feedback circle.

With 360-degree feedback, the assessment of an individual's strengths and development needs is more reliable and valid because of multiple raters. Multiple raters provide different perspectives on an individual's performance, making the feedback more accurate and more useful to the recipient. By collecting feedback from several different individuals with different relationships to the recipient, the effect of personal biases is significantly decreased.

Many different labels are given to 360-degree feedback. Some of the more common ones include multi-rater feedback (or assessment), multisource feedback, multipoint feedback, upward feedback, full-circle feedback, and peer feedback. Some of these labels reflect the different aspects of 360-degree feedback (see Exhibit 1.1). For example, upward feedback refers to feedback from direct reports (subordinates). True 360-degree feedback, however, involves providing ratings from (at least) the person whose performance is being rated and his or her boss, peers, and direct reports.

Exhibit 1.1.
Components of the CCL 360-Degree Feedback Process

Multiple people provide ratings for an individual. Supervisors, peers, direct reports, the participant, and others complete valid and reliable surveys on which they rate (or assess) the behavior and other attributes of the participant using numerical rating scales. The ratings are collected anonymously (that is, the participant cannot tell who provided the ratings), with the exception of supervisor ratings. Because most people have only one boss, it is difficult if not impossible to keep supervisor ratings anonymous.

Reports and interpretation are provided. Participants receive feedback reports that itemize the results of the assessment. With the assistance of a professional feedback coach, participants examine their high ratings (strengths) and low ratings (weaknesses), as well as the differences between their own and others' perceptions of their performance.

Participants create a development plan. Feedback coaches work with individuals who have received the feedback to identify ways those participants can change their behavior to become more effective leaders.

Important characteristics of CCL's 360-degree feedback process include ownership of the data, accountability of the participants, credibility and commitment, communicating expectations, and continuous learning.

Ownership of the Data

The ownership of a participant's data is an important issue in the 360-degree feedback process and is directly related to maintaining the confidentiality of the data. Participants and raters are more likely to provide honest ratings when they know the data will remain confidential (Brutus & Derayeh, 2002). One of the critical characteristics of developmental feedback is that each participant "owns" his or her data. CCL believes that 360-degree feedback data should not be shared with participants' organizations unless the participants decide to do so themselves.

In 2001, CCL surveyed 395 organizations that purchase management and leadership development services. Included in the survey were 212 CCL clients and 183 non-client organizations. Following is a summary of the survey results related to ownership of the data (Bradley, 2001).

- A total of 56 percent of respondents indicated that employees own the data from their 360 processes. Responses from clients and non-clients were not significantly different.

- Overall, 65 percent of respondents said employees were not required to share their data with the organization. The majority of CCL clients (78 percent) indicated that employees were not required to share their data, while 62 percent of non-clients reported that employees were not required to share their data.

In the CCL 360-degree feedback process, the feedback reports are sent directly to a trained facilitator, who meets with the participant in a private consultation. The participant and the coach are the only people who see the participant's individual data, unless the participant decides to share it with others.

If the purpose of the 360 assessment is for development, CCL recommends that a feedback coach be used. The coach can be an external consultant who is an expert in facilitating feedback or an internal HR professional who has been trained to provide 360-degree feedback. A number of studies report that the use of feedback coaches to facilitate the feedback has a more positive effect on both the leader and the organization (see, for example, Luthans & Peterson, 2003; Smither, London, Flautt, Vargas, & Kucine, 2003). Atwater, Brett, and Charles (2007) caution against providing participants with feedback reports without facilitated feedback assistance. Participants who work with a coach are more likely to set goals, share the feedback with their bosses, and improve their ratings on a subsequent 360 administration (Smither, London, Flautt, Vargas, & Kucine, 2003).

Brutus and Derayeh (2002) report that every organization in their study that failed to meet the objectives of the 360 process had failed to facilitate the feedback process. In these organizations, participants received reports in the mail without individual or group facilitation with a trained feedback coach. The organizations that were successful in meeting their objectives for the program were the ones that facilitated the feedback process. Facilitation sessions are critical to help participants identify goals for needed behavior change.

Accountability of Participants

Because the participant owns the data, and the organization does not see the results, the participant is accountable for acting on the feedback by creating and carrying out a development plan. In the development plan, the participant notes areas of strengths and areas in which development is needed. Then, with the assistance of the feedback coach, the participant develops a plan to address the areas for development.

Credibility and Commitment

The 360-degree feedback process must be seen as credible by the participants in order to gain their commitment to change their behavior.

For the feedback to be credible, at least four factors must be present (Van Velsor, 1998):

1. Trust in the process must be built by protecting the quality of the ratings and ensuring the anonymity of the raters and the confidentiality of the participants' data (Antonioni, 1994; Brutus & Derayeh, 2002). Anonymity means that the identity of the raters is protected—their identity remains unknown to the participant and others. Confidentiality, on the other hand, means that the feedback report is available only to the participant and the feedback coach, unless the participant decides to share it with others.

2. The process should focus on important developmental goals rather than on superficial change. In other words, the process must not only measure observable behaviors but also allow the participant to link these behaviors to effectiveness on the job.

3. The process must be understood by all involved—by both the raters and the participant. Instructions should be unambiguous, and the questions on the survey should be clearly written. Clarity also includes stating and supporting confidentiality of the data and the anonymity of the raters.

4. Finally, the 360-degree feedback must be directly linked to developmental planning in order to gain a commitment to behavior change from the participants.

Communicating Expectations

An effective 360-degree feedback process allows the organization to promote important values by communicating what behaviors are expected from employees. For example, an organization can communicate the importance of commitment to good customer service by allowing customers to provide feedback directly to employees (Testa, 2002). Customers can be broadly defined as any individual who experiences the employee's behavior.

Continuous Learning

CCL believes that effective 360-degree feedback encourages continuous learning on the part of the participants. Just receiving the feedback will not necessarily make a person a more effective leader—the change must come from within. It is important, therefore, first to "unfreeze" the participant's self-view so he or she will be willing to change behaviors. The best way to unfreeze the self-view is to provide the participant with accurate data from multiple perspectives and to encourage openness in accepting the feedback. For 360-degree feedback to be effective in enhancing participants' self-awareness and in encouraging them to engage in self-development, it must be embedded in a larger development process that includes a development plan and organizational support for employee development, such as coaching (McCauley & Moxley, 1996).

Participants who receive support from their organizations for development-related activities have more positive attitudes toward the 360 process and are more likely to be involved in developmental activities (Maurer, Mitchell, & Barbeite, 2002).

HOW THE CCL 360-DEGREE FEEDBACK PROCESS WORKS

The person being assessed selects a number of coworkers to participate in the feedback process. Working individually, the raters and the participant complete surveys designed to collect information about the participant's specific skills, behaviors, and other attributes that are important to managerial or leadership effectiveness.

After the raters complete the surveys, their ratings are sent either electronically or by postal mail to a centralized location for scoring. A report is produced and delivered to a feedback coach, who then meets with the participant to review the report. The coach can be someone external to the organization or an internal HR professional who will keep the feedback report confidential. The coach is trained to interpret the results of the particular instrument being used and helps the participant understand what the various scores mean. The coach helps the participant use the feedback to create a development plan geared toward increasing the participant's effectiveness. The surveys, reports, and development plans can be printed materials, delivered electronically, or can be a combination of media.

WHY 360-DEGREE FEEDBACK IS NEEDED

In the life of a busy organization, people often find themselves starved for feedback. Two factors play into this. First, people become caught up in day-to-day pressures and responsibilities and fail to pick up the cues from others that provide one source of ongoing feedback. Consider this all-too-familiar scenario: While waiting for the elevator after a tough meeting, a manager gets a pat on the back from his colleague for handling a presentation well. The next day, someone lets him know that his reaction to a sensitive question was unnecessarily defensive. At the end of the week, one of his team members cautions him that his instructions to their assistant sounded patronizing. These small bits of data—informal feedback—float around managers all the time, largely unattended in the rush of business concerns.

Formal 360-degree feedback provides something that informal feedback seldom does: a structured means of collecting and processing data, and an opportunity to reflect on this valuable information (see Exhibit 1.2). It may be the only time some leaders ever consciously stop to take stock of their performance effectiveness in an organized way.

A second factor that impacts an individual's access to meaningful feedback is that giving and receiving feedback can be perceived as threatening activities (they may *actually* be threatening, in some instances). Often people in organizations think that giving and receiving feedback is not worth the risk.

Contemporary organizations pay a lot of lip service to the need to increase communication in all directions; at the same time, many people are reluctant to give performance feedback to coworkers, especially to their superiors. When they ask themselves, What do I have to gain by telling my boss about his development needs? they struggle for an answer. The higher up in the organization one moves, the less feedback one receives (Kaplan, Drath, & Kofodimos, 1985).

Formal 360-degree feedback, by its nature, helps reduce the interpersonal threats of face-to-face feedback for both parties. The formalized structure and the neutral character of the instruments provide a format for objectivity. The formal feedback process also focuses on the valid assessment of behaviors that that organization values.

THE IMPORTANCE OF MULTIPLE PERSPECTIVES

Receiving feedback from only one person is rarely sufficient to create positive change in the participant. Whether the message is about a strength or about an area for improvement, the participant may wonder whether one individual's opinion constitutes valid and complete information. Yet the most common example of feedback in the workplace is that of a supervisor giving feedback to a direct report (see Exhibit 1.3).

Even though interpreting their significance sometimes takes work, multiple views from a 360-degree process are preferable:

- They reflect a more comprehensive representation of a manager's reality, in which a multiplicity of views has to be taken into account.

- They reduce the potential for bias (see, for example, London & Beatty, 1993).

- The boss alone often does not observe the individual's behavior daily, especially if the individual is located in another building, another region, or another country, a familiar situation that makes it very difficult to maintain an accurate ongoing assessment.

Exhibit 1.3.
Providing Effective Feedback on the Job with SBI

Few managers are skilled at giving constructive feedback. Effective feedback requires a different pattern of communication from the one most people have learned through experience. To be effective, a manager has to learn specific interpersonal skills and exercise the discipline to use them. In the busy workplace, many managers don't bother. And when feedback is perceived as criticism, most people are not likely to accept what their managers have to say.

To increase the quality and effectiveness of feedback, CCL recommends using the three-step process it teaches and practices: the **situation-behavior-impact method (SBI)**. This simple feedback method keeps comments relevant and focused to increase their effectiveness. With SBI, you describe the situation in which you observed the other person (it could be a boss, a peer, a direct report, or even a family member), the behavior you observed, and the impact of that behavior on you in that situation.

- The increase in team-based work and flatter organizations dictates the need for collecting and synthesizing feedback from team members and others who may not be members of the participant's immediate work group.

- Previously untapped sources of feedback can be included; for example, the effectiveness of some leaders can be judged by how well they work with people outside the organization, such as customers, suppliers, or clients.

Despite these advantages, 360-degree feedback can result in the participant receiving a variety of responses based on each rater's perspective. Unanimous agreement, even if less than complimentary, is easy for the participant to understand. But such agreement is seldom the case. It is more common for participants to be perceived differently by different raters (see Exhibit 1.4). This variance can cause considerable confusion for participants, unless they are able to think through the reasons with the help of a trained feedback coach.

Exhibit 1.4.
Feedback Variations Among Multiple Raters

There are many valid reasons why feedback is not uniform (McCauley & Moxley, 1996). It may be that the participant actually behaves differently with different people. The amount of exposure that the participant has with different groups also explains variations. For example, one group may have more opportunities to see the participant displaying the behavior being rated.

Also, the raters' expectations come into play. Raters may have differing expectations about how the participant will use the specific behavior when interacting with them, and so they have their own opinions as to whether the behavior, or its absence, is a problem.

Finally, two raters can interpret the same behavior very differently. For example, a manager is blunt in his interpersonal interactions. One rater interprets the behavior as direct, efficient, and precise. Another rater sees the same behavior as abrupt or even rude. Helping with this analysis is one of the functions of the debriefing session between participant and feedback coach.

THE ROLE OF 360-DEGREE FEEDBACK IN THE LEADERSHIP DEVELOPMENT PROCESS

What are organizations trying to accomplish when they implement a formal 360-degree feedback process? As you might imagine, their goals are as diverse as the organizations themselves. Each frames and focuses its efforts in different ways.

Some organizations use 360-degree feedback primarily as part of development processes for individual managers and leaders (for CCL's position, see Exhibit 1.5). For example: A manager is struggling with providing direction and vision for his group; he can see the value but isn't clear on how to go about it. After completing a 360-degree feedback instrument that contained the item, "Brings up ideas about the future of the organization," he realizes from his raters' responses that his focus with them—measured by the amount of time

---

Exhibit 1.5.
CCL's Approach to Feedback for Development

CCL uses 360-degree feedback solely for developmental purposes to provide the most accurate data possible to its participants. CCL's philosophy toward 360-degree feedback is shaped by three lessons it has learned from working with leaders and from our research on leadership development (McCauley & Moxley, 1996).

1. People can learn, grow, and change to become better leaders. There is ample evidence for this. People are not born to be good leaders; becoming a good leader requires hard work and learning.

2. Self-awareness is the cornerstone for leadership development. Any development as a leader (or as a person, for that matter) begins with taking an open and honest look at one's strengths and weaknesses.

3. Development is an ongoing process closely related to one's work. The challenges in a person's work drive the person to learn and grow, so you cannot expect to send someone to a single training program and have him or her return "fully developed." However, such events can play an important role in the development process if they are closely linked to the challenges of the work situation.

---

spent—was always on tactical issues. He thought he was helping them work toward goals; they thought he was not sharing long-range guidance. Armed with this new perspective, this manager can change his behavior and become more effective in setting direction for his group.

Even when people have solid insights about their own strengths and development needs, they may not be aware of how these qualities affect their coworkers day to day. Consider this scenario: An international high-tech manufacturing organization frequently sends individual managers one at a time to a leadership development program conducted by an outside company. At this program, the participants take part in an elaborate business simulation and receive feedback on their behavior from the other twenty people in the program. After the simulation, participants receive the results of their 360-degree assessment from their coworkers back home. The participants are surprised at the consistency of feedback from these two sources. They now have a clearer idea of how consistently their behaviors affect others.

Organizations may also focus 360-degree feedback on developing individuals in particular subgroups (for example, high-potential managers) or at different times in a manager's career (such as prior to a promotion or near the completion of a developmental assignment).

In addition to its use in developing individual competency, organizations also use 360-degree feedback to determine group strengths and development needs. For example, by compiling individual feedback results into an aggregate group profile, one large industrial construction company focuses on the competencies that, as a company, it would like to maintain or develop further. The resulting information is built into every manager's development objectives for the upcoming year. Taking this example one step further, some organizations use the group data to establish needs for organizational training activities.

Some organizations use 360-degree feedback initiatives to broaden employee awareness of valued behaviors (see Exhibit 1.6). The simple process of reading and answering the specific items on the feedback instrument puts these valued dimensions out in front of people and usually triggers discussion. For example, a large European insurance company decided that the key to its survival was to be less bureaucratic and more entrepreneurial. It used a 360-degree feedback instrument designed specifically to measure behaviors known to exist in successful entrepreneurial environments. It implemented this process with its senior managers first, then cascaded it down through its new managers.

Another example comes from the telephone industry. One service provider decided that, as a market edge, it was going to pursue excellence in customer service for its data and voice subscribers. But many of its managers had been hired in the telephone monopoly era, when customers did not have options and were forced to live with the service they received. This company started a major initiative that included conducting internal customer-service workshops; individual coaching; pushing decision making downward in the organization; and completing 360-degree feedback to focus on decisiveness, customer focus, and responsiveness.

Exhibit 1.6.
How 360-Degree Feedback Supports Organizational Values

The use of 360-degree feedback can support three types of organizational values: open communication, valuing employee input, and setting the expectation that people should take charge of their careers. Here are some illustrations.

- A major urban hotel group wants to encourage open communication among its owners. One part of its approach is to initiate a regular 360-degree feedback process in which each of the six participants is a rater for all the others. This surfaces issues for discussion and helps establish an open-door work environment. By asking others to complete the survey, these leaders are indicating that they are amenable to performance feedback. They are, in a sense, establishing a norm for communication.

- An organization becomes particularly interested in using a 360-degree feedback instrument as part of its efforts to enhance employees' sense of empowerment. The process of multi-rater assessment is inclusive; soliciting participation from diverse rater groups indicates that the organization is interested in their perspectives.

- An international consumer products company encourages its managers to actively plan their career progression from the day they are hired. The company uses 360-degree feedback to put data in the managers' hands and responsibility for career planning on their shoulders.

As a result, the company was able to help its managers see where their skills did or did not match the organization's valued behaviors.

ADMINISTRATIVE VERSUS DEVELOPMENTAL USE OF 360-DEGREE FEEDBACK

An important factor to consider when implementing 360-degree feedback is the purpose for conducting the assessment. Will the results be used for performance appraisal, which has an administrative (or decision-making) component, or will they be used solely for developmental purposes? The types of decisions that will be made with the results will have a significant impact on how the process is carried out (Bracken, 1996).

In general, there are two schools of thought about the use of 360-degree feedback instruments. Organizations that employ 360-degree feedback instruments for administrative purposes use them primarily to make decisions about hiring, promoting, or compensating people. While 360-degree feedback administered for administrative purposes often has a developmental component, it is often a secondary consideration. By comparison, organizations that use 360-degree feedback instruments for development only use the data to help participants create a plan to increase their effectiveness in the organization.

The critical difference between these two approaches is the ultimate ownership of the data. In assessment for administrative purposes, the organization owns the data. In assessment for development, the participant owns the data. While the participant is encouraged to work collaboratively with his or her boss to construct a development plan, the feedback report itself is confidential and seen only by the participant, with the exception of the feedback coach. Ultimately the participant decides if, with whom, and how he or she shares the report data.

Feedback for Performance and Selection

The use of 360-degree feedback for administrative purposes, such as performance appraisal, selection, and compensation, remains controversial (Bracken, Dalton, Jako, McCauley, & Pollman, 1997). Data from the Upward Feedback Forum indicate that 93 percent of the organizations that were surveyed used 360-degree feedback for developmental purposes, and half of those also used it for administrative purposes (Timmreck & Bracken, 1995). Of those using 360-degree feedback for administrative purposes, about half stopped using it for various reasons, including negative employee reactions (Timmreck & Bracken, 1997).

In a survey of over one hundred organizations, Brutus and Derayeh (2002) found that 74 percent of organizations were using 360-degree feedback for developmental purposes, while 26 percent were using it for administrative purposes or a combination of both developmental and administrative purposes. Brutus and Derayeh noted, however, that in some organizations, ratings supposedly collected for development only somehow found their way into the hands of individuals responsible for making administrative decisions.

When 360-degree feedback is used for performance appraisal, competencies are assessed that are directly related to the job in question. The items on the instrument are focused on the participant's current position rather than on developing competencies for future assignments. In performance appraisals, the instrument is usually shorter than one used for development.

When an instrument is used for development, its content is more developmental in nature; that is, it assesses the participant's potential to perform at a higher level. When used for developmental purposes, the instrument may be longer and cover competencies that can be targeted for development.

When using 360-degree feedback for performance appraisal, an organization should be able to readily demonstrate that the assessment instrument is related to the job in question. One way to do this is to ensure that the competencies being measured are important for successful performance on the job.

When the 360 assessment is used for employee selection, the organization must deal with critical legal issues. For example, it may be necessary to conduct a validity study to demonstrate that the ratings are directly related to job performance, or that the ratings have no adverse impact on protected classes of employees. This requires that the data be maintained so it will be easily accessible for validity and adverse-impact studies.

It is also important that 360 instruments used for development are demonstrated to be reliable and valid measures of the competencies of interest. Instruments that are used for purely developmental purposes, however, do not face the same legal requirements that pertain to instruments used for administrative decision-making purposes.

When a 360-degree feedback process is conducted for administrative purposes, the organization owns the data, which it uses to make decisions about the individuals being assessed. Depending on the purpose of the assessment, however, different people in the organization will have access to the data. If the purpose is for selection, the hiring manager and relevant HR staff will have access to the data. If the purpose of the administration is succession planning, the executive team may be allowed to see the data. In any case, it should be made clear upfront to the participants exactly who will have access to the data. Furthermore, it is important to maintain the confidentiality of the data. Only people who have a legitimate need to see the data should have access to it.

The confidentiality issue is not trivial. Evidence indicates that rater responses change when they know the participant's feedback data will be made public (London & Smither, 1995). The effects of allowing the ratings to be seen by the organization can be significant. For example, it's easy to see that employees might rate themselves differently if they know their bosses will see their data (Dalessio, 1998). There also may be similar effects on the ratings of others—managers may be less inclined to identify areas for development for their employees if they know others may see the ratings.

For a 360-degree process to be its most effective, anonymity for certain rater groups is critical. Because anonymous raters have been found to be more honest than identified raters, more accurate ratings can be expected when anonymity can be ensured (Kozlowski, Chao, & Morrison, 1998). If the raters begin to believe that their anonymity will be compromised, then less honesty can be expected in future.

The bottom line is that 360-degree feedback processes must be carefully designed to suit the purpose of the assessment. Although feedback collected for administrative purposes can be used for developmental purposes, systems designed for these purposes are usually not appropriate for use as development tools, and vice versa (Fleenor & Brutus, 2001).

Feedback for Development

Another importance difference between using 360-degree feedback for developmental purposes versus administrative purposes is the type of goals that are set. With developmental purposes, learning goals are set. These goals typically involve development of competence. Performance goals set for administrative purposes, such as performance appraisal, usually involve meeting certain objectives directly related to the achievement of results on the job.

Research suggests that raters will change their ratings if they know their ratings could affect the participants' salary or promotion opportunities. Waldman, Atwater, and Antonioni (1998) found that up to 35 percent of raters would change their ratings if the ratings were used for administrative purposes.

According to London (2001), 360-degree "feedback can be used for both developmental and administrative purposes, but this takes time" (p. 383). He believes, however, that 360 feedback works best when used, at least initially, for developmental purposes only. Organizations that initially use 360 feedback for administrative purposes often find there is a lack of trust of the process among employees (Atwater, Brett, & Charles, 2007). Brett and Atwater (2001) suggest that organizations implementing 360-degree feedback should first focus on the developmental aspects of the process.

CCL's bias is that the primary goal of feedback is individual development, and it has designed instruments and processes to support this goal. Using 360-degree feedback for administrative purposes requires different data collection and feedback processes. Therefore, CCL recommends that feedback collected for developmental purposes not be used for administrative decision-making processes.

When 360-degree feedback is used only for developmental purposes, participants should receive the feedback in a psychologically safe environment. This includes a feedback coach who has been trained to present negative information with a great deal of sensitivity. Trained feedback coaches are also able to deal with any defensiveness or denial on the part of the participant.

The bosses' ratings are also a critical component of the development process. For example, bosses are the best source of importance ratings for the competencies on which participants' effectiveness is rated. Additionally, the boss may be in a better position than the other raters to understand fully the organizational context in which the participant's performance occurs. For example, the boss may be aware that certain constraints in the organization may have prevented the participant from accomplishing some goals.

Finally, in a developmental 360 process, participants are encouraged to share high-level feedback with their bosses. For example, they may want to let their bosses know on which competencies they were rated relatively high and on which they were rated relatively low.

IMPLICATIONS

Receiving feedback that is contrary to one's self-image can be stressful and threatening. The more discrepant the information, the more stressful it is. As summarized by Dalton (1998), "Using 360-degree feedback as part of the appraisal process represents naiveté to issues of hierarchy, status, and retribution and violates the condition of psychological safety that is necessary for a person to receive dissonant information about the self."

According to Brutus and Derayeh (2002), around 20 percent of organizations do not link their 360-degree feedback processes with other developmental systems. CCL integrates 360-degree feedback into its leadership development programs because we believe that feedback must be embedded in a larger development process to be effective for developing leaders.

This chapter presents some of the considerations to be made before implementing a 360 process in an organization. We describe the distinct difference between developmental and administrative use and state CCL's approach to using 360 for development only. The subsequent chapters describe using a development approach in a 360-degree initiative.

Implementing a 360-Degree Feedback Process

There are several important parts to implementing an effective 360-degree feedback process, and through practice we have seen that following this outline can dramatically increase the odds of a successful 360 initiative:

- Establishing goals for the 360 initiative
- Assessing individual and organizational readiness
- Designing the process
- Selecting or designing a tool
- Identifying and preparing participants
- Preparing the organization
- Administering the assessment and processing the results
- Delivering feedback
- Supporting development
- Evaluating the process

This chapter covers the first seven topics (goals through assessment administration and processing results). Chapters 3 and 4 offer guidance on delivering feedback, supporting development, and evaluating the process. In addition, these later chapters include information about leveraging group reports, following up, and ensuring 360-process success. Exhibit 2.1: Considerations for Implementing

Exhibit 2.1.
Considerations for Implementing a 360-Degree Feedback Process

Business Need

- The reasons for conducting this process are clearly linked to my organization's business needs.
- The type of behavior change we want to encourage is clear.
- We have specified the expected outcomes for the process.
- We know who the target population is.

Organizational Culture

- We have specified the intended purpose of the process (for development or for evaluating performance).
- The process fits in the organizational context.
- Trust and openness are present in my organization.
- The process has integrity, anonymity, and confidentiality.

Competencies

- The items and scales of the instrument make sense.
- The dimensions are relevant to my organization.
- My organization has an underlying management model.
- The assessment dimensions are related to my organization's management model.

Reliability and Validity

- The collected data is meaningful to the participant; it is consistent and accurate.
- The instrument assesses what it claims to.
- The ratings from the instrument are related to effectiveness as a manager, leader, and other organizational roles.
- The assessed behaviors are amenable to change.

a 360-Degree Feedback Process will help you think through those issues that are important to a successful implementation.

SETTING GOALS FOR 360-DEGREE FEEDBACK INITIATIVES

Before choosing a feedback instrument, an organization must identify the business purpose and the target population. When you set out to design and deliver a feedback intervention, get clear answers on these four questions:

1. Why do we need this?

2. Why right now?

3. Who is it for?

4. What outcomes do we expect?

Use Exhibit 2.2 as a place to note your answers.

A common mistake that organizations make is to commit to an assessment activity of some kind without clearly defining what they hope to gain from it or connecting it to specific business needs. It might seem that every other organization on the planet might be employing some type of 360-degree feedback, but that does not mean it is the right thing for your organization to do. If you are unable to define a business issue that you can resolve using 360-degree feedback, you will be unable to measure whether or not you have been successful.

To ensure that all of the stakeholders are in agreement on the purpose, it is important to set goals for the assessment initiative. What is the intended purpose of the intervention? The type of decisions that will be made with the results will have a significant impact on how the process is carried out (Bracken, 1996).

CCL recommends that the goal of the 360-degree feedback process be to develop the leadership capabilities of your organization's employees. To meet this goal, you will need to implement a process that meets confidentiality and anonymity requirements, select an instrument that will provide accurate and meaningful feedback to your participants, and provide feedback to the participants. The organization also must provide support to the participants in carrying out their development plans.

ASSESS ORGANIZATIONAL READINESS

For a 360-degree feedback process to be effective in meeting its goals, it is important to determine your organizational readiness. One crucial factor is the level of trust in the organization. For the process to be successful, there first must be a culture of trust and openness in your organization. Otherwise, people will not feel secure in providing the authentic feedback that is required for developing leadership skills. Some other questions to ask regarding your organization's readiness include the following:

- **What are the expected outcomes?** The most likely outcome is the development of your managers—the identification of their strengths and weaknesses to position them for development planning.

- **Who is the target population?** Usually 360-degree feedback is used to assess managers, but the process can also be used to assess individual contributors, with ratings being gathered from the bosses, peers, and customers. Decide at the start who the target population will be.

- **Are the expectations realistic?** If stakeholders expect to see immediate behavior change after the participants read their feedback reports, then the organization may not be ready.

- **Does your organization currently have an underlying management model?** To increase the odds of success, the competencies on the feedback instrument should be directly linked to the underlying management model of the organization. The management model consists of those leadership competencies that are considered important for effective performance in your organization. If the instrument does not reflect your organization's management model, the feedback process might be off-target.

- **Does the 360-degree feedback process fit the organizational context?** Will the culture of your organization support the rating of managers by their direct reports? If not, a great deal more effort will be required to prepare the organization for the implementation.

- **Is there sufficient organizational commitment?** Does upper management demonstrate strong support for the process? Is the organization willing to commit to full and open disclosure of the process at all levels of the organization?

- **Are there other factors that might influence the success of the process?** For example, has there been a recent experience with a 360-degree instrument that might shade people's perceptions of the process?

- **Do you plan to provide formal training for participants and raters?**

You can use Exhibit 2.3 to summarize your findings about your organization's readiness for a 360 process.

The advent of Internet-based surveys has changed the data-collection process dramatically. More than 90 percent of CCL's assessments are now completed online. Implementing a web-based 360-degree feedback process is clearly a

Exhibit 2.3.
Organizational Readiness Worksheet

Date:

- What is the level of openness and trust in the organization?

- What are the expected outcomes of the 360 process?

- Who is the target population?

- Are the expectations realistic?

- Does the organization currently have an underlying management model?

- Does the 360-degree feedback process fit the organizational context?

- Is there sufficient organizational commitment?

- Are there other factors that might influence the success of the process?

- Do we plan to provide formal training for participants and raters?

cost-effective alternative to other methods (for example, paper and pencil, phone, or fax). If you choose an online assessment tool, additional readiness assessment may be necessary. The following factors should be included in your readiness assessment for web-based 360 feedback (Bracken, Summers, & Fleenor, 1998).

- **Prior 360 feedback experience.** If employees are accustomed to the traditional 360 feedback process, the transition to web-based 360 will be easier. Respondents typically find that the web eases administrative burdens inherent in traditional methods: rater nomination, survey administration, and reporting. Additionally, the web is secure and confidential. Raters who felt "exposed" using other media where the ratings are collected and stored in-house may be more comfortable using the web.

- **Accessibility.** Accessibility to the Internet may be your organization's single most significant obstacle. The efficiencies of a web-based solution section are greatly reduced when a significant portion of an organization's workforce does not have direct Internet access through their own computers at work or at home. An option for these organizations is to provide kiosks that non-connected employees can use.

- **Familiarity.** While completing a survey on the web may not seem particularly challenging, it can be a daunting experience for new or novice users. Even experienced users will become frustrated if the process is not clear, easy to navigate, and tolerant of mistakes and lost connections. If your organization already uses the web for other applications, such as for benefits enrollment or job postings, you are an ideal candidate. Employees will most likely be comfortable using the web for these other purposes, making the addition of 360 feedback a minor step.

- **Culture supports technology.** Organizations that embrace technology are quicker to welcome a web-based 360 process. Some organizations are embracing technology as a means to achieve competitive advantage. At the other end of the continuum, some organizations are technology "averse" or have a senior management team that resists change.

- **Organization demand.** One of the more desirable environments is when an organization that is already using paper-based 360 feedback demands that the process be moved to the web. These organizations are typically experienced users who have seen the immediate benefits of the web after having used less efficient technologies.

- **Technical sophistication.** Technical savvy can be a double-edged sword. As organizations and their employees become more educated and aware of the pros and cons of different technologies, users begin to raise questions around issues such as security. The designers of 360 feedback systems need to ensure full security and confidentiality for their users and also educate and communicate the features of the system that protect the confidentiality of the data.

- **Adequate IT resources.** The amount of assistance required from an internal IT (information technology) group will vary from project to project. IT support will probably be most crucial during the early phases of the project when the system is being accessed for the first time. For example, employees with old versions of browsers may need to upgrade them. One critical need is an accurate list of e-mail addresses for all participants, and for as many of the potential raters as possible.

- **Geography.** One of the compelling benefits of a web-based solution is global access. The web provides worldwide access with cost-effective and instantaneous data access. Companies that are geographically dispersed, with global sites, will see a substantial advantage to web-based application.

- **HRIS database.** Depending on the way the 360 process is implemented, it may be necessary to access the HR information system (HRIS) to identify participants, demographics (for example, department, location), and reporting relationships (supervisor, subordinate, peer). Having a reliable, up-to-date HRIS will be invaluable.

Use the Online Readiness Worksheet (Exhibit 2.4) to rate your organization on each of these factors.

Exhibit 2.4.
Online Readiness Worksheet

Factor	Low	Medium	High
Prior experience	No prior experience	One or two administrations and/or only part of company	Three or more administrations, entire company
Commitment to ongoing use	No plans beyond current administration	Plans for at least one more cycle	Integrated into HR systems requiring its ongoing use
Accessibility	Little or no access to Internet from inside company	About 50 percent have some access to Internet	Over 80 percent can access Internet
Familiarity	Little if any reason for employees to use Internet	Use of Internet encouraged	Use of Internet required for other systems
Cultural support of technology	Significant resistance to using technology	Some new technologies recently introduced	Technology advances seen as competitive advantage
Organizati-onal demand	No organizational demand	Able to recruit a group for pilot program	High demand for the service from the entire organization
Comfort level	Perception that someone could hack into data	Perception that Internet is reasonably secure	Perception that Internet is more secure than other media
IT resources	No commitment from IT	IT availability on as-needed basis	Full-time dedicated IT resources
Geography	Single location	Multiple domestic locations	Multiple worldwide locations
HR information system (HRIS) data	No HRIS database	HRIS database often unreliable	HRIS database comprehensive, well maintained

Source: Adapted from Bracken, Summers, & Fleenor, 1998.
Leveraging the Impact of 360-Degree Feedback. Copyright © 2008 by Center for Creative Leadership. Reproduced by permission of Pfeiffer, an Imprint of Wiley. www.pfeiffer.com

DESIGNING THE PROCESS

The next step in implementing an effective 360-degree feedback process consists of planning and design. You will need to make several decisions at this stage:

- Who will fill the necessary roles, such as vendor contact, administrator, and participant point of contact

- How and when you will start the process, establish a calendar including what the milestones are, when the deadlines occur, and how the individual participants can monitor their rater return rates in process

- How to conduct a pilot test by determining the size of the pilot group, the individuals to include, whether to start at the top and roll it down, or some other approach

- How to ensure the support of upper management by consulting and involving them very early in the process and by tying the initiative to specific business goals.

Aside from addressing these important issues, other decision points come into play during the design phase, such as the following:

- What type of behavior change does the organization want to encourage? Does the organization want to change specific management-related behaviors, such as delegation, or does it want to change broad-based leadership behaviors, such as acting systemically?

- Does the process have integrity? How will anonymity and confidentiality be ensured?

- Who owns the data? Will only the participant and the feedback coach see that individual's data, or will others in the organization, such as the participant's boss and the HR staff, also see it? If so, this describes an administrative (not developmental) process.

Gain Upper Management Buy-In and Direction

Support from the top of your organization is crucial to a successful 360-degree feedback process. Following are some common concerns that upper management may have that you should be prepared to answer:

- How does 360-degree feedback improve productivity?
- Does 360-degree feedback reward "nice" people who don't work hard?
- Do some people refuse to change after receiving the feedback?
- Is there really much difference between 360-degree feedback and supervisor appraisal?
- Isn't it too expensive and time-consuming?
- Will employees use deliberate manipulation, sabotage, and unresponsiveness when the data is used for decision-making purposes?

SELECTING OR DESIGNING A 360-DEGREE FEEDBACK INSTRUMENT

Your organization's business needs should drive your decision about what kind of instrument to select. A manager's performance is defined within the context of a business strategy, and the selection of an appropriate instrument should also be. Several different types of 360-degree instruments are available (off-the-shelf, online, and customized, for example). Familiarize yourself with their features prior to selecting which one your organization will use (see Exhibit 2.5).

All too often, HR executives or consultants will choose a particular 360-degree feedback instrument simply because they have an affinity for it and try to use it in all cases. They would be better off putting their energy into clearly defining the

---

Exhibit 2.5.
Sources for Selection

A comprehensive source for selecting a suitable 360-degree feedback instrument is *Choosing 360: A Guide to Evaluating Multi-Rater Feedback Instruments for Management Development* (Van Velsor, Leslie, & Fleenor, 1997). To familiarize yourself with what is available, consult *Feedback to Managers* (Leslie & Fleenor, 1998), which provides basic descriptive and technical data on 360-degree feedback instruments available for use for leadership development.

---

need for assessment, and then finding the best instrument for that purpose. If the purpose of the feedback intervention is to focus the participants on organizational competencies, for example, then the instrument selected should ask questions that connect to that competency model.

Once you have defined the business need for the assessment, the next step is to identify the target population. This is essential for choosing the right instrument. People at any level can benefit from 360-degree feedback, but you should take care to ensure that the instrument is appropriate for the participants' particular situation. For example, an instrument containing many questions about managerial and supervisory skills would not be an effective tool for assessing individual contributors or support staff.

Managers need different kinds of feedback at different times in their careers. Early on, they might use 360-degree feedback to help define what skills are important. Later in their careers, they want to know how their strengths and weaknesses affect others. As they move higher in the organization, it may be critical to use 360-degree feedback to evaluate their ability to set and implement a vision for the company's future success.

The first step in narrowing your selection is to find an instrument with psychometric integrity. It should be professionally developed and adequately tested. Use the Instrument Integrity Checklist (see Exhibit 2.6) to compare the instruments you are considering. The publisher or provider of the instruments should be willing and able to supply answers.

Be a savvy consumer. Ask the provider for a report of the research behind the instrument. Obtain samples of the survey and feedback report. The individual items should make sense to you, and they should reflect behaviors that your organization values. The provider should have a depth of expertise in creating research-based assessments—not just experience in using the assessment as a way to sell its consulting services.

Other things to investigate include accompanying materials and technical support. Is there a developmental planning guide to help participants sort their data and set a workable plan for change? Does the organization have adequate resources to respond to questions or problems encountered in using the instrument? The Selecting a Feedback Tool Checklist (Exhibit 2.7) can help you work through all of the issues related to choosing the appropriate tool for your organization.

Exhibit 2.6.
Instrument Integrity Checklist

Date:

Instrument:

- What evidence is there that the instrument is a valid and reliable measure of competencies that are important for the organization?

- How do we know that it really measures what it claims to measure, and that the resulting scores are empirically related to effectiveness on the job?

- What evidence is there that the instrument is reliable? That it is stable over time?

- How do we know that the items within a scale (dimension or competency) measure the same construct?

- What is the level of agreement within rater groups?

Exhibit 2.7.
Selecting a Feedback Tool Checklist

The steps in evaluating a 360-degree feedback instrument are laid out sequentially here. All steps are not equal in complexity or importance—we suggest that you make the most critical decisions early in the process. This way, you can save some effort by eliminating instruments that don't meet your needs in terms of content and that don't pass muster when it comes to reliability and validity.

Date:

360-process target population and goals:

Step 1: Find out what is available.

_____ Conduct a thorough search of management and leadership development tools currently available commercially.

_____ Review *Feedback to Managers* (Leslie & Fleenor, 1998) for instruments that may meet our needs.

Step 2: Collect a complete set of materials.

____feedback reports

____technical manuals

____supporting materials (development guides, for example)

____purchasing information, including price

Step 3: Match an appropriate tool to organization.

____a good fit with our organization's leadership model

____a good fit with our target audience (the level of employees who will receive feedback)

Step 4: Familiarize myself with how the tools were developed.

The items (questions) on the tools were developed from

_____theory

_____research

_____experience

The items are

_____behavioral

_____skill based

_____trait based

The method used to develop the feedback scales was

_____statistical analysis

_____a conceptual approach

Step 5: Assess the tool's quality.

Consult the user's manual for each feedback tool to determine its quality.

_____Are the scores produced by the tool consistent (reliable)?

_____Does the tool measure what it claims to measure (that is, is it valid)?

_____Does the content of the instrument appear to be appropriate for use in our organization?

_____If the instrument is to be used internationally, has it been translated into the appropriate language and back-translated into our native language to ensure the accuracy of the translation?

(Continued)

Exhibit 2.7. (*Continued*)

Step 6: Evaluate the display used in the feedback report.

_____Is there a graphic display?

_____Is there a narrative display?

_____Is the report understandable?

Step 7: Learn what strategies are used to facilitate the interpretation of scores.

_____comparison to norms

_____highlighting largest self-rater discrepancies

_____item-level feedback

_____highlighting high/low scores

_____comparison to ideal

_____importance to job or success

_____"do more/do less" feedback

Step 8: Look for development and support materials.

What kind of support material is there for the manager's development?

_____development guide

_____goal-setting worksheets

_____workshop available

_____vendor hotline

_____other (describe)

What kind of trainer/facilitator support is available?

_____trainer's manual

_____workshop

_____overheads

_____access to subject-matter experts

_____other (describe)

Is certification required?

_____yes

_____no

How is scoring done?

_____self-scoring

_____by the vendor

_____by computer software installed locally

_____online (web-based)

Step 9: Consider cost.

_____The price of the tool compares favorably to others that are similar.

_____It is within my organization's budget.

Step 10: Consider the time it will take to complete the instrument.

_____How many items does the instrument contain?

_____Is it too long to be useful and accepted by our managers?

Adapted from Van Velsor, Leslie, & Fleenor (1997).

STANDARDIZED OR CUSTOMIZED INSTRUMENTS

An organization can choose an existing, standardized assessment instrument (sometimes called *off-the-shelf* solutions) or have an instrument custom designed for its use. Unfortunately, there is no such thing as the perfect instrument, and there are advantages and disadvantages to both types.

A primary advantage to using a standardized instrument is cost; it is often less expensive than a customized alternative. Also, an existing 360-degree feedback instrument can provide extensive normative data, so participants have the opportunity to compare their scores to many other managers in other organizations.

Standardized Tools

Standardized instruments have been created to be sold directly to individuals or organizations that wish to implement 360-degree feedback. The availability of off-the-shelf instruments is increasing at a rapid pace. If you decide to use such an instrument, your first task is to learn what instruments are available in order to choose the best possible tool for your organization. Use the Standardized Instrument Checklist (see Exhibit 2.8) to record your notes about the standardized feedback tools you are considering.

Customized Tools

An alternative to using an off-the-shelf instrument is to create a survey specifically designed for the organization. A customized instrument has an advantage over a standardized one in that it is designed to measure competencies that are important and specific to the organization (Chappelow, 2004).

At first glance, this may seem to be the best choice. An organization is like a family: it likes to think that it is unique in its best qualities and in its dysfunctions, and that no off-the-shelf instrument can capture its particular essence. While it is not difficult for an organization to come up with a list of important competencies, the difficulty lies in creating the survey, scoring program, and developmental materials that are needed for a successful 360 process.

In addition to the logistical challenges of creating a customized instrument, validity and reliability studies must be conducted to ensure that the instrument is psychometrically sound, that is, reliable and valid. (Reliability is the consistency or stability of the data collected by the instrument; validity is the extent to which the instrument measures what it is supposed to measure and the appropriate use

Exhibit 2.8.
Standardized Instrument Checklist

Date:

Instrument:

_____The items and scales make sense to our organization (they have face validity).

_____The competencies the instrument assesses are relevant to the behaviors we want to change in our organization.

_____The competencies it assesses are related to our organization's underlying management model.

_____The data will be meaningful to our managers. It will be perceived as consistent and accurate.

_____The behaviors assessed are amenable to change.

_____The provider has suitable experience and expertise with the instrument, target audience, and subject matter.

of the results.) Some organizations fail to conduct these studies; however, this approach is extremely shortsighted. If the organization expects its employees to be open and to make changes based on the feedback, it must provide evidence that these changes are actually the ones that are needed.

Demonstrated reliability and validity are essential for an effective and defensible 360-degree feedback process. It's counterproductive to give employees feedback that is based on unstable and inaccurate data. Designing a reliable and valid survey requires the involvement of an expert in instrument development. A doctoral degree in psychology, educational measurement, or a related field is usually required. If the organization doesn't have this expertise internally, it may have to hire the services of a consultant who has the necessary training and experience.

Much of this expense and difficulty can be avoided by using a customizable instrument offered by a provider of 360-feedback services. These instruments allow the selection of desired competencies from a collection of competencies that have been tested for reliability and validity. The content and length of a customized instrument can be tailored by selecting important competencies and combining them to create an assessment that closely reflects the needs of the organization. All of the guidelines that apply to selecting an off-the-shelf instrument apply to customizable instruments, and you can use the Customizable Instrument Checklist (see Exhibit 2.9) to expand your analysis of instruments you are considering.

**Exhibit 2.9.
Customizable Instrument Checklist**

Date:
Instrument / Provider:
- Does the application require both paper and online options, and does the assessment provide both options?

- What customization options exist?

- Can e-mails and greetings be personalized?

- Can the website be branded for your initiative?

- Is the software hosted or must you install it at your site?

- What are the technology requirements to access and use the software?

- What administrative capabilities are available to you?

- How is project status monitored?

- What report options are available?

- How long does it take to set up your survey once customization choices have been made?

PREPARING THE PEOPLE INVOLVED

Every person involved in the assessment and feedback process should be adequately prepared for his or her role. The purpose for the 360-degree feedback initiative and the expected outcomes should be explained fully, and it should be made clear how the feedback will be used.

As an example of how such preparation might work, consider the case of a regional electric utility that holds a half-day orientation session to kick off the assessment phase of its development program for upper managers. The participants who are to receive feedback, their bosses, and their raters attend this session together. The president of the company introduces the background and goals of the overall program. The senior HR executive then introduces the 360-degree feedback instrument and discusses its purpose. Raters are given instructions to reduce rating errors, and screenshots of the web-based user interface are demonstrated. The bosses or coaches of the participants attend an additional afternoon session that helps them understand how to best support the developmental planning process.

Preparing Senior Management

Once an organization has selected an instrument to use, it must provide the proper structure to help the participants collect the best data possible.

Frequently, organizations are ill-prepared for what lies ahead, especially if their senior leaders have not experienced 360-degree feedback before or if they have experienced a less-than-successful implementation. To prepare your organization, conduct a briefing for the executive team. Your agenda might include the following:

- Discuss the business drivers for the feedback and development process.
- Describe the leadership framework of skills, perspectives, and capacities that will be assessed in the process.
- Describe the roles, responsibilities, and expectations of the participants, managers, and organization.
- Introduce and describe an overview of the 360 project plan and/or process.
- Identify the integration points to other people management processes.
- Outline next steps and implementation schedule.
- Share sample materials and outputs (optional).

Identifying and Preparing Participants

The organization should choose participants according to the business need for the assessment. People at any level of the organization can benefit from 360-degree feedback, and individuals need different feedback at different times during their careers (Chappelow, 2004). For example, new employees need feedback on which skills are important to their jobs, while mid-level employees require feedback on their strengths and developmental areas. As employees move up the organizational ladder, they require more feedback on their ability to create a vision for the organization's success.

Be sure to provide the participants with some type of orientation to the 360-degree feedback process. The example outlined above is a fairly typical example of a participant orientation session. A sample presentation for an orientation session can be found in Appendix A.

The single most common question among participants is, "Who should I select to be my raters?" The participant typically collects feedback from the boss, peers, direct reports, and a catch-all category called "others." Some 360-degree instruments also allow for rater groups such as superiors or board members. The instrument provider usually suggests the optimal number of raters for each group; a typical distribution is one boss, five peers, and five direct reports. The most accurate responses come from raters who have had a chance to observe the manager's variety of behaviors over time. Therefore it is most beneficial for the participants to select raters who know them well and know their work.

Some organizations prefer to control distribution of surveys by selecting the raters for the participant. However, this could undermine the participant's openness to the resulting data. A better approach is to let the participant select the raters. Alternatively, the organization may supply a list of required raters to the participant and let the participant decide who, in addition, he or she will include.

To ensure that you have covered all the significant steps in participant and executive preparation, use the checklist in Exhibit 2.10.

Data Confidentiality

The data collected through assessment-for-development instruments belong to the individual participants. It should be the participant's decision whether or not anyone else reviews the feedback report. Breaches of confidentiality, even if accidental, can jeopardize the feedback process, compromise the integrity of the people who administer the organization's development program, and lead to a

Exhibit 2.10.
Participant and Organization Preparation Checklist

Date:

360-process initiative:

____We have received endorsement for the initiative at the highest levels.

____We have conducted a presentation or other orientation to the 360 process for participants.

____We have explained to the participants how they were selected for this process.

____We have explained the milestones and deadlines involved.

____We have explained to the participants and their facilitator that the feedback reports will be confidential.

____Participants have been instructed to select raters who know them well and who have had the opportunity to observe a variety of their behaviors over time.

____ We have conducted an executive briefing.

____ We have linked the initiative to specific business goals.

____ We have a clear communication plan in place with the participants and raters.

____ If there have been any recent similar initiatives that failed, we have determined how to do things differently this time around.

mistrust of subsequent assessment activities. Take the utmost care throughout the entire feedback process to protect these data.

Even though paper-and-pencil surveys are still available through some providers, the vast majority have moved online. Protecting the data in this environment requires commonsense safeguards such as password access and unique rater and participant identification using login names or similar entries.

Choosing and Preparing Raters

Just as critical as preparing the participant is preparing the raters to provide useful feedback. A rater is someone who completes a survey on behalf of the participant on a 360-degree instrument. This person should have worked with the participant during the past year and be able to provide appropriate feedback.

Two components help to ensure quality ratings: (1) using raters who have the ability to accurately assess and evaluate the behaviors measured and (2) preparing these individuals to provide accurate ratings. Rater training can help prevent errors in providing accurate feedback. Specifically, training can help reduce recency errors (ratings based on most recent experiences) and halo errors (generalizing ratings across items—for example, rating an individual high on all items because he or she is outstanding on one particular item).

One aspect of preparing raters consists of exposing them to the scales and items before they are asked to provide responses. Typically referred to as *competency scale training*, this type of training can increase rater accuracy. Another type of preparation, *frame-of-reference training*, involves calibrating each scale by using a list of behaviors that correspond to performance levels in the organization (that is, what constitutes effective and ineffective behaviors in the organization). The checklist in Exhibit 2.11 summarizes the major considerations in choosing and preparing raters.

Rater Perceptions   Raters are likely to have sensitivities to the 360-degree feedback process that may affect the results, including:

- Perceptions of the instrument
- Thoughts about how and why they were chosen as raters
- Expectations about the outcomes of the process
- Perceptions of their anonymity
- Perceptions of the return on the time they are asked to invest

You can manage these sensitivities by educating raters about the competencies, providing examples of behaviors associated with the competencies, working to improve observational skills, explaining how they were selected to be raters, and explaining the outcomes of the process.

Exhibit 2.11.
Rater Preparation Checklist

Date:

360-process initiative:

____We have explained to raters how they were selected and what the outcomes of the process are to be.

____We have provided rater training to help prevent errors in providing accurate feedback.

____Our rater training included competency scale training (a review of the 360 instrument's scales and items).

____Our rater training included frame-of-reference training (matching each scale to a list of behaviors that correspond to performance levels in the organization).

____We have described to raters how they can provide ongoing support to the participant.

____We have clarified for raters how anonymity issues will be handled.

Explain the Outcomes of the Process   Raters are asked to invest time in the development of others, and it is important to consider what raters might expect in return. These outcomes may include the following:

- Increased awareness of performance and work-related behaviors
- Increased awareness of raters' expectations
- Greater alignment of performance expectations between employees and the organization
- Improved communication about work expectations
- Improved work behavior

One goal of a 360-degree feedback process is to provide participants with information about strengths and areas for development. Remind raters that they must provide information in both areas. After reviewing the feedback, participants should send their raters follow-up notes thanking them for helping with their development. Afterward, the participants may decide to share with their raters the insights, goals, and challenges that resulted from receiving their feedback. Change rarely occurs overnight, nor does it occur in a vacuum. Help raters understand that they can help by providing ongoing support to the participant.

Clarify Rater Anonymity   The sensitive nature of personal feedback requires that you protect the privacy of the raters. If the raters suspect that their feedback is not anonymous, they may be reluctant to participate in the process or may shade their answers. Two areas in which your efforts will engender active participation are in clarifying anonymity and in buttressing the confidence in the feedback itself.

Anonymity means that no one will be able to tell which feedback a particular rater provided. It is a safeguard to ensure that the information gathered is candid and accurate. Many raters are concerned about retaliation or punitive consequences for their ratings, especially when the person they are rating is their boss. Explain whose scores will be anonymous and whose will not be. Anonymity usually is ensured by averaging the individual ratings within a particular rater group (direct reports, peers, and so on) and by not reporting the ratings for a group unless the actual number of raters exceeds a minimum number (usually three).

Construct your questionnaires (or evaluate the instrument you select) so that participants cannot tell who said what on their reports. CCL does this on our assessments by requiring a minimum of three respondents in the rater categories of "peers" and "direct reports." If three or more people from within the same category return surveys, their answers are combined and presented as an aggregate score. If fewer than three people in one category return surveys, then the participant's report does not include item-level feedback in that category. A common exception is with the boss's feedback. This data is frequently identified separately. In this case the materials should give the boss clear notice that his or her responses are not anonymous.

Research shows that anonymous raters are more likely to provide accurate, objective feedback than are their counterparts who are required to identify themselves (Kozlowski, Chao, & Morrison, 1998). If the raters believe that their anonymity will be compromised, then less honesty can be expected in future administrations of the 360 process (Bracken, Timmreck, Fleenor, & Summers, 2001).

Some instruments provide a way for raters to add written comments, expanding their feedback to include data that the instrument does not capture. These broader, deeper impressions can be quite helpful to a participant, but at the risk of losing anonymity (see Exhibit 2.12) because the participant may be able to identify the rater's communicative style.

ADMINISTERING THE ASSESSMENT AND PROCESSING THE RESULTS

The assessment process should be administered in a manner that is consistent and fair for all participants and raters. The data collection and processing should be both efficient and cost-effective (Bracken, Timmreck, Fleenor, & Summers, 2001).

Exhibit 2.12.
Tradeoffs of Written Commentary

Written comments from raters may introduce *verbatim bias*. In its work facilitating one-on-one feedback sessions, CCL has noticed that sometimes participants give more attention to written comments than to numerical or graphical scores. No matter what their scores on the standardized part of the assessment, some people tend to focus on and remember the written comments more. As a result, verbatim comments that are seemingly inconsistent with the numeric results can unfairly bias the feedback. Feedback facilitators should help participants put these comments in perspective if written responses are included in the 360-degree process. On the other hand, written comments allow a rater to provide feedback that might not otherwise surface within the limitations of the survey questions.

The feedback report should contain clear information as to how the recipient is perceived by his or her raters. If appropriate, the report may contain statistical comparisons to others in the organization and industry norms from outside organizations. The final feedback package should be delivered in a sealed envelope. It should contain a summary of the feedback, including the questions responded to by the raters, directions for interpreting the results, and action-planning worksheets. We go into the details of delivering the feedback in the next chapter.

Delivering Feedback

To successfully deliver feedback, experienced coaches should help the recipients reach their own conclusions about the data. The feedback coaches should also make sure the recipients understand the process. They should help the recipients to go past the data to the meaning and assist them in understanding that conflicting views can be valid.

Three common approaches to delivering feedback are one-on-one sessions, group sessions, or a combination of the two. The choice of method often depends on the type of instrument used, the organization's plan for its implementation, and the number of participants involved in the initiative.

FACILITATING A GROUP FEEDBACK SESSION

If you are working with more than one participant, it's usually more economical to have the participants go through introductory steps in a group setting. In this setting you can provide an introduction to the 360-degree instrument, distribute individual feedback reports, and introduce the idea of planning development. Group sessions are less staff-intensive and afford the opportunity to use small-group activities when appropriate to enhance learning. The significant disadvantage is that the participants do not have an opportunity to speak privately with a coach to discuss their data.

A group feedback session is most often intended to adequately prepare participants to receive and understand their individual feedback. Ideally this session would be kicked off by a senior executive from the organization. A basic outline of steps would include the following:

- Clarify purpose, goals, and expectations of the feedback process.
- Briefly discuss the research that supports the 360-degree feedback instrument being used.
- Provide a context for receiving feedback, including the following points
  - First, feedback is data, and the data are neutral. Data cannot make decisions about you. You make decisions about the data.
  - This is just one snapshot of you. It does not define you as a person. It is important that you put this snapshot alongside others to see what overarching patterns emerge.
  - People often make one of two common mistakes when they receive 360-degree feedback: they accept the information too quickly, or they reject it too quickly. Consider it; think it over.
  - You are the expert about you. You know who filled out the questionnaires, you know your work situation. The coach will help you understand the data, but you must decide what they mean.
- Explain how to read and interpret the report using a sample report to have the participants do some "armchair analysis."
- Distribute their personal feedback reports to them.
- Allow time for individual reflection on the data, and for answering questions.
- Introduce any data-sorting exercises included with the materials. CCL feedback reports come with a developmental planning guide that contains a variety of exercises that help the participants group and interpret themes and patterns in their data.
- Explain the logistics of the one-on-one sessions, if they are scheduled.

Exhibit 3.1 is a sample agenda covering all of these points.

Exhibit 3.1.
Sample Group Feedback Session Agenda

Organization:

Date:

360-Degree Feedback Process

Purpose, goals, and expectations

Supporting research

Feedback report overview

Sample report analysis

Participant feedback reports/Q&A

Interpretation exercises (optional)

One-on-one logistics (optional)

FACILITATING A ONE-ON-ONE FEEDBACK SESSION

In the one-on-one approach, a participant has an individual session with a feedback coach who includes a brief introduction to the background of the instrument, an interpretive session about the participant's data, and further assistance with developmental planning.

Even instruments that are fairly simple and straightforward (such as CCL's SKILLSCOPE, for example) are enhanced by a private consultation with a coach who has experience using the instrument. Because of this, and as a condition of responsible use, some providers require that you use a one-on-one feedback session with their 360-degree instruments. One-on-one feedback sessions are particularly important for participants receiving feedback for the first time. They typically appreciate the opportunity to open up and discuss their feedback, whether it's good or bad news, with a dispassionate third party.

The feedback coach should have training and experience with the particular instrument being used; some providers require they be certified in its use. Ideally, the coach is someone who is objective and outside the participant's chain of command or influence. For example, one large pharmaceutical firm maintains a pool of eight independent consultants to deliver instrument feedback as part of its leadership development program for middle managers. The company finds that this gives the process additional credibility, since the organization is investing in experts. It reinforces the confidential nature of the data, because no company employees (even those in HR) see the participants' reports. The organization also benefits from using the same consultants, who over time become familiar with the issues and goals of the organization.

It is important to give participants ample time to analyze their data before the one-on-one session. For the sake of efficiency, it is tempting to hand participants their reports, give them a few minutes to digest the data, and then shuttle them off to the one-on-one session. When this happens, participants arrive for the feedback session still trying to understand what the information in their hands means. With no time to reflect on the numbers, graphs, and tables in the report, they may not yet be ready to consider the data's full implications.

For example, if some of the feedback is negative or surprising to the participants, it is likely that when they begin the one-on-one session they are still dealing with their emotional reactions to the data or to the raters. It is difficult for the feedback coach to move things beyond the emotions and to closely analyze the data. It is better to give participants an overnight break between receiving the feedback and having the one-on-one session. If they have a chance to sleep on the data, they usually understand it better, have time to deal with their immediate emotional reactions, and are more open and positive in the one-on-one sessions. Keep in mind that feedback data does have a shelf life, and that the one-on-one session should occur within one to four days of receiving the data.

Schedule one-on-one sessions in a private office or other room. The coach prepares for the session in advance by reading the person's report thoroughly and making notes. Feedback coaches should give participants the option to make an audio recording of the session so that they can be fully engaged with the feedback coach rather than writing notes. This also serves as a useful tool when reviewing progress against their development plans in the future.

A good feedback coach tries to understand not only the data but also the context for the particular person. This is best achieved by asking the participant a few short questions at the beginning of the session.

- *How do you want to use the data?* The person who is seeking a promotion to the next level in the organization has an entirely different framework for feedback than does a person who is happy in her current role and wants to enhance her working relationship with her direct reports.

- *What is happening in your present job situation?* There may be something unusual going on within the company that is having an impact on the person's feedback.

- *Were you surprised by any of your feedback? Disappointed? Pleased?* Sometimes these questions alone are enough to get people talking about their reactions to the data.

- *What overarching themes do you see emerging from your data?* Perhaps the most valuable thing experienced feedback coaches can do is help participants make connections in the data that they do not initially see.

- *How would you summarize your data? What are the key strengths? What are the key development areas?* Helping the participant summarize and focus the data is critical. The session should progress from the global to the most specific.

- *What changes are you motivated to make right now? In the future?* The most critical decision the participant makes about the data is choosing the areas on which to focus and work.

Experienced feedback coaches use their expertise about the instrument, but they resist the temptation to act as an expert on any particular participant's data. The participants are the experts, deciding for themselves what to pay attention to and how to make meaning of the feedback.

Coaches are commonly asked, What do you think my raters meant by this response? Although they can make an educated guess, they really have no way to know the answer to that question. Effective feedback coaches see themselves as guides to the data, asking helpful questions and helping the participants see connections in the information they have received.

COMBINING FEEDBACK SESSION TYPES

Combining the group session and adding one-on-one sessions provides the optimal outcome to feedback delivery. In this scenario, the introductory presentations are made once in a group setting, and the individuals meet one-on-one with a coach to discuss their personal data privately. From its practice, CCL knows that the value of the session is greatly enhanced if the participants have substantial time to review and reflect on their data. Facilitators of group sessions should be prepared to remain in the meeting room after the group to provide short, informal "walk-up" sessions for participants with immediate concerns or questions about their reports.

LEVERAGING GROUP REPORTS

A group report is a snapshot of the group from which it was derived and should not be generalized beyond that group. As with individual reports, you should use precautions to protect the anonymity of individuals within the group as well as of the group itself. Keep the following points in mind when using a group report.

- The group is entitled to view the results of its own data.
- The group report data should not be shared with other groups to whom the group might be compared without permission of the group unless the group identities have been made anonymous. Each group member should be told where results will be shared outside the group.
- Do not use group reports to discriminate against demographic groups or individuals.
- Group reports must be interpreted very carefully.

When participants reach their own conclusions about the data they receive, they create a personal investment in their own development. Experienced feedback coaches can help guide that process, and they can help recipients go deeper to the meaning behind the numbers.

Ensuring 360-Degree Feedback Success

Providing 360-degree feedback to participants is only the beginning of the development process. Individuals sometimes confuse assessment with development, but it is what happens *after* the assessment that matters most to organizations. Development is the actual sustained behavioral change that leads to an increase in the individual's effectiveness. Feedback should not be seen as the sole developmental event, but as an unfreezing of the participant's perceptions of the development process. To move from this shift of perspective to a change in behavior, you can bolster the feedback program several ways. One is to foster support from your organization and the participant's boss for developmental work. Another is to help participants create realistic, robust development plans. Leveraging group reports, evaluating the 360-degree feedback process, and following up with participants also helps extend the learning begun in the initial assessment phase.

ORGANIZATIONAL SUPPORT

Many organizations spend a great deal of time and money on conducting the assessment phase of 360 feedback, but fail to provide organizational support for participants to partake in developmental activities (Atwater, Brett, & Charles, 2007).

Healy, Walsh, and Rose (2003) found that the majority of organizations in their survey did not require follow-up activities to 360 feedback. Only 20 percent of these organizations required participants to discuss their feedback with their bosses.

Follow-up developmental activities after feedback, however, are critical. Participants who receive developmental support from the organization report more positive attitudes toward the feedback and are involved in more developmental activities after receiving the feedback (Maurer, Mitchell, & Barbeite, 2002).

Reinforcing 360 feedback with training or coaching enhances its benefits. Research shows that participants who work with feedback coaches are more likely to set specific goals and ask ideas for improvement from others (Seifert, Yukl, & McDonald, 2003); they also tend to receive higher follow-up ratings from bosses and direct reports (Smither, London, Flautt, Vargas, & Kucine, 2003). Additionally, participants who are involved in training programs or developmental activities such as coaching are more likely to improve than those who do not (Hazucha, Hezlett, & Schneider, 1993).

How can you tell whether your organization supports development? In such organizations, there are expectations for continuous learning and growth. Organizations that authentically support development show several signs of that commitment. Which of the indicators in the Organizational Support for Development Checklist (Exhibit 4.1) are true in your organization?

According to Atwater, Brett, and Charles (2007), there are a number of specific actions organizations should take to provide sufficient support for a successful 360-degree feedback process, including the following:

- Doing more than just suggesting that participants engage in developmental activities and coaching
- Encouraging participants to hold follow-up discussions with bosses and direct reports
- Providing support for developmental activities following feedback
- Being aware of the positive impact of the feedback on participants and the organization beyond individual awareness and development
- Using feedback in conjunction with training or coaching to have a more positive impact on the participant and the organization
- Facilitating the feedback process

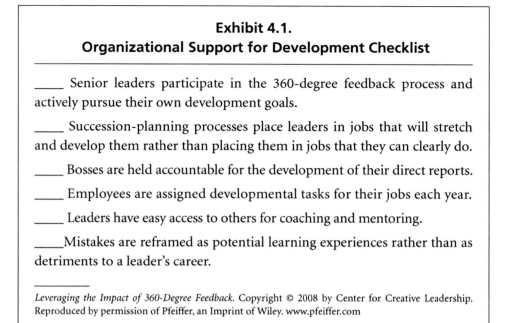

Exhibit 4.1.
Organizational Support for Development Checklist

_____ Senior leaders participate in the 360-degree feedback process and actively pursue their own development goals.

_____ Succession-planning processes place leaders in jobs that will stretch and develop them rather than placing them in jobs that they can clearly do.

_____ Bosses are held accountable for the development of their direct reports.

_____ Employees are assigned developmental tasks for their jobs each year.

_____ Leaders have easy access to others for coaching and mentoring.

_____Mistakes are reframed as potential learning experiences rather than as detriments to a leader's career.

_____

GETTING AND USING THE BOSS'S SUPPORT

At a minimum, participants in a 360-degree feedback initiative should solicit the endorsement and support of their bosses or, as an alternative, a feedback coach. Managers who have bosses who support the changes necessary for their development are more likely to achieve the necessary results (Hazucha, Hezlett, & Schneider, 1993).

Participants should share what they have learned through feedback, clarify their development plans and goals, and talk about how their bosses can help with the development process. Bosses should follow up with their direct reports who have been through a 360-degree feedback process and let the direct reports know that they want to play a role in the development process. Some ways in which bosses can contribute include the following:

- Helping participants narrow their focus on what to work on

- Suggesting and supporting possible developmental assignments

- Helping establish behavioral milestones and check-in points

You can use the example (a process put into play at an international pet food company) in Exhibit 4.2 as a guide to creating an approach for helping the participant's boss support development. It follows a simple model of three boss-and-participant meetings that work well for this purpose.

Exhibit 4.2.
Sample Plan for Creating Boss Support for the 360 Process

Meeting 1. Before completing the assessment forms, the participant meets with the boss or coach to

- Discuss how the participant plans to use the information collected by the assessment (for example, to work more effectively with direct reports, to identify the next job challenge)

- Set a date for the next meeting, to take place after the participant receives the feedback report and has a one-on-one consultation with a feedback coach

Meeting 2. After the participant receives feedback and has had an opportunity to identify development goals, the participant meets with the boss or coach to

- Gain any clarification needed (in a non-defensive manner) from the boss about specific questions regarding the boss's feedback (which would apply only when the 360-degree feedback instrument has the boss's scores broken out separately)

- Share with the boss the development goals the participant chooses, to elicit buy-in and support of the effort

- Set a date and time for the next meeting (should be approximately six months later)

Meeting 3. The participant and boss meet after six months to

- Discuss the progress made toward the development goals (which can be refined or redirected by the participant if necessary)

- Set a date and time for another progress check in six months

DEVELOPMENT PLANS

A 360-degree feedback activity is not a stand-alone event. The feedback by itself probably does not have a long-lasting effect or lead to behavioral change. In fact, providing assessment without developmental planning and follow-up almost guarantees that the organization does not receive its money's worth. As one senior manager from a large bank stated, "We have access to some of the best 360-degree feedback instruments on the market through our human resources office. The problem is, nothing happens afterward. You are on your own to try to guess how best to carry on. Your boss may even hold you back. We even have a name for it; we call it 'drive-by assessment.'"

To keep a drive-by assessment from occurring in your organization, devote some critical time and resources to the most important follow-up to feedback: the development plan. Through this plan, participants identify important goals for improvement and develop strategies for meeting these goals. The goals should be important, specific, relevant, and focused on behaviors that can be changed or skills that can be learned.

Development Goals

It is better to limit the number of goals than to try to work on too many goals at once. Deciding which goals to work on can be difficult, so once participants have considered how to approach their development and identified development goals, they should ask themselves three questions:

1. Does the goal motivate and energize me?
2. Will achieving this goal help me be more effective in my current position?
3. Will my organization benefit from my achieving this goal?

Quality developmental planning is, of course, more than just setting individual goals. It is a thorough blueprint for achieving and sustaining behavior change by using a variety of strategies proven to enhance learning. Using the feedback collected from a sound 360-degree feedback instrument, a person can select a theme on which to focus. Exhibit 4.3 shows a series of questions for participants to consider in choosing their developmental focus.

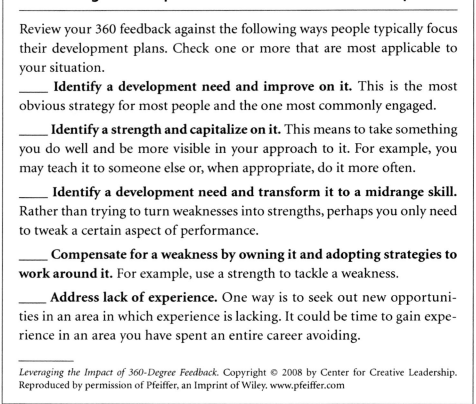

Exhibit 4.3.
Choosing a Developmental Focus: Checklist for Participants

Review your 360 feedback against the following ways people typically focus their development plans. Check one or more that are most applicable to your situation.

_____ **Identify a development need and improve on it.** This is the most obvious strategy for most people and the one most commonly engaged.

_____ **Identify a strength and capitalize on it.** This means to take something you do well and be more visible in your approach to it. For example, you may teach it to someone else or, when appropriate, do it more often.

_____ **Identify a development need and transform it to a midrange skill.** Rather than trying to turn weaknesses into strengths, perhaps you only need to tweak a certain aspect of performance.

_____ **Compensate for a weakness by owning it and adopting strategies to work around it.** For example, use a strength to tackle a weakness.

_____ **Address lack of experience.** One way is to seek out new opportunities in an area in which experience is lacking. It could be time to gain experience in an area you have spent an entire career avoiding.

Leveraging the Impact of 360-Degree Feedback. Copyright © 2008 by Center for Creative Leadership. Reproduced by permission of Pfeiffer, an Imprint of Wiley. www.pfeiffer.com

Learning Strategies

Once a participant has identified an appropriate goal, he or she should use a variety of strategies to achieve the goal. It's common to meet an eager participant, sincerely motivated to make behavioral changes as a result of a formal feedback event, who when setting out to plan for personal change asks, Can you recommend a good book (or workshop) on this subject? But CCL's research shows that very few leaders actually reported learning important lessons through reading books. One study indicates that reading and coursework account for only 6 percent of the events that teach the key managerial lessons (McCall, Lombardo, & Morrison, 1988). By using only this approach, the individual is closing himself or herself off to the richest kind of developmental activities.

It would be much more effective to set a development strategy that takes into account a broad variety of experiences. CCL's research and experience emphasize that learning strategies fall into three broad categories: experience, ongoing feedback, and role models and coaches.

Practice   Participants need time to practice their new skills and behaviors. If there are few opportunities to practice in the current job, the participant should identify other ways of adding such challenges, such as being assigned to a cross-functional task force.

New Job Assignments   When practical, new jobs with different duties (starting something from scratch, fixing something gone wrong, moving from a line to a staff job, or accepting a broad change in scope and scale of responsibilities) can teach a wide variety of important lessons.

Existing Jobs   There may be tremendous potential for development in someone's present job. By becoming aware of the challenges in their current roles and how these challenges can teach critical lessons, people are in a better position to capitalize on them and address development needs quickly.

Your developing leaders can also identify what new jobs or assignments could help them further develop; however, these experiences should not be limited to the workplace. There are also volunteer experiences in the community that can provide the necessary challenges.

Ongoing Feedback   A critical component of any development plan is to build in progress checks. This feedback may be formal or informal, but the plan should provide for collecting it regularly. As the participants practice their new skills and behaviors, they must have ongoing feedback about how they are doing. Each participant should identify at least one person who can provide candid, helpful, and specific feedback. The participant should talk with this person at regular intervals to obtain specific feedback.

Developmental Relationships   The best free developmental opportunity most people have is the opportunity to watch someone else do something well. For example, if a person decides to work on delegating more effectively, he or she should identify someone who does it well. Then he or she should take every opportunity to observe that person in action and try to discover what makes him or her effective. It would also help to engage that person in ongoing conversations about this subject. The aid of a coach, one who knows the development goals and can give advice and support, should also be considered.

Training and Reading   Although training and reading constitute a small part of the sum total of developmental learning, they remain important. Books and training programs can provide expertise and strategies for developing in targeted areas. Skill-building training programs often provide a safe place to practice new behaviors because the consequences are minimal, and participants may be willing to take more risks in trying new behaviors and skills.

A fully realized development plan that ties individual goals to organizational needs, and in that process uses a 360-degree feedback activity to develop capabilities and capacity, will go a long way toward getting your organization a good payoff for its investment. CCL's Developing Leadership Talent program is a helpful guide to such an approach, which is detailed in a book (Berke, Kossler, & Wakefield, 2008).

Integrating for Continuous Learning

Developing leaders should employ multiple strategies to maximize their learning. They also should integrate their development plans with their work, rather than viewing them as separate from one another. This is often a new way of thinking for some individuals. They may think of development as something that is done away from the job and that detracts from their work. Leaders, however, may learn the most through the challenges they face at work. After reflecting on their learning experiences, leaders should be able to see that they need to consciously shape their work experiences into opportunities to learn.

FOLLOW-UP

Participants should be held accountable for their progress toward meeting the goals they have set during their feedback sessions. This includes follow-up meetings with the raters who provided feedback, follow-up with the boss who assisted in setting the development goals, and follow-up with the feedback coach. Goldsmith and Underhill (2001) report that managers who held follow-up feedback sessions with their raters showed significant improvement in their effectiveness as leaders. They also found a positive relationship between the frequency of follow-up and perceived positive change. This study, along with others, underscores the importance of following up as a way to positively alter perceptions of effectiveness.

EVALUATING THE PROCESS

As with any process, it is important to assess the impact of 360-degree feedback. CCL recommends a four-step evaluation process.

1. **Evaluation planning.** Develop evaluation objectives. Provide feedback or evidence regarding the impact of 360-degree feedback initiatives. Inform curriculum development efforts and/or initiative improvement. Investigate the connection between leadership and organizational impact. Match evaluation objectives with solutions.

2. **Data collection.** Collect information using questionnaires, interviews, focus groups, observation, and performance reviews. Other sources you can use for collecting data about the 360-degree feedback process come from individual and group action plans, customer input, self-assessments, assessments from peers and bosses, and information gathered from coaching sessions.

3. **Data analysis.** Examine the extent to which the 360-degree feedback ratings correlate to performance outcomes valued by the organization. Think about how your organization can improve the 360 component of the leader development initiative to increase its impact.

4. **Reporting.** In any report of a 360 process, include an executive summary, a description of the evaluation deliverables and evaluation questions, an overview of how data were collected and analyzed, a data summary organized by evaluation questions and important themes, recommendations, and a copy of the tools used to collect data.

Exhibit 4.4 contains a detailed framework for evaluating 360-degree feedback. Readers may also want to consult *Evaluating the Impact of Leadership Development* (Hannum & Martineau, 2008), which offers advice for carrying out a robust measurement of development initiatives such as 360-degree feedback.

Exhibit 4.4.
A Framework for Evaluating 360-Degree Feedback

Levels of Evaluation	Research Questions	Key Outcomes Assessed	Who Is Assessed	Type of Assessment	Approximate Time Frame
Level 1: Reaction	What did participants think of the 360-degree feedback process? What did they plan to do differently as a result of the 360-degree feedback?	Relevance and usefulness to actual work practice; perceived value to the learner and stakeholder; perceived transferability of the training to the workplace	Participants who received feedback	Questionnaires, interviews, focus groups	Immediately after feedback
Level 2: Learning	What did participants learn as a result of the feedback?	Learning process effectiveness; competency awareness; increased self-awareness; action planning; development strategies	Participants who received feedback	Before-and-after questionnaires; written test or exercises; performance demonstrations; peer assessment; skill-building exercises	Two to six months after feedback

Level	Question	Measures	Who	Method	Timing
Level 3: Application	Did participants change their behaviors based on the feedback? Which development strategies are most effective for leadership development?	Changes over time; group effectiveness; organizational commitment	Participants who received feedback; their coworkers and bosses	Interviews, questionnaire	Three to six months following completion of the training
Level 4: Business impact	Did the change in behavior positively affect the organization?	Impact on job performance; overall effectiveness; retention; career development; time and cost factors	Bosses of managers who received feedback, stakeholders	Interviews, questionnaire	Ten months following completion of the training

Source: Adapted from Kirkpatrick's (1975) Four Levels of Training Evaluation

Current Issues and Future Directions for 360-Degree Feedback

D espite its long history, the process of using 360-degree feedback for development has not settled into a complacent, accepted practice. Several issues are still debated within the community of HR professionals, providers, researchers, scholars, and others about its use, its place in development, and its effect. Three important issues are the merits of re-administering 360-degree feedback instruments over a period of time, the usefulness of creating norms among participants in a 360-degree feedback process, and what it means to have agreement or disagreement between rater and participant responses.

In addition, there are several trends that may influence the design and use of 360-degree feedback processes in the future. These trends include a shift organizations are making toward customized instruments and away from off-the-shelf solutions, and the growing use of comments to add to the numerical ratings.

RE-ADMINISTERING ASSESSMENTS

The re-administration of 360-degree feedback involves having the participants go through the process again after a period of time (after one year, for example). There are advantages and disadvantages to re-administering surveys. Advantages include the ability to spot development trends in individuals and groups, and disadvantages include (1) raters having different expectations the second time around, which influences their feedback and (2) changes in the organization that may affect how the feedback is interpreted when the instrument is used at two points in time.

Advantages

There are definite benefits to re-administering a 360-degree feedback survey. The re-administration will allow the recipients to focus on trends by comparing the data from the two surveys. This can be valuable in helping the participants determine whether they have improved in the areas targeted for development. Re-administration can provide valuable training evaluation data by tracking the progress in groups of employees over time. It also encourages feedback recipients to make self-development a continuous process. CCL recommends that 360-degree feedback become an ongoing process that is administered on a regular basis throughout the organization.

Disadvantages

There is an old adage: When you measure something, you change it. *Instrument reactivity* refers to the way an instrument reacts when it is administered to the same people a second time. This may be particularly true in the case of a 360-degree feedback instrument. Because both the participants and raters have experienced the process before, they may react differently than they did the first time around. For example, raters may expect that the participants have improved their leadership effectiveness as the result of going through the development process. This expectation may result in the raters being stricter when providing their ratings. So participants who have actually improved their leadership effectiveness may be rated the same or even lower than they were in the initial assessment.

Temporal validity is the term used when referring to organizational changes that occur between two uses of a 360-degree survey. After a time of change, results may be interpreted differently when a survey is used a second time. For example, an organization may have gone through a transition such as downsizing, which again may result in the raters being more stringent in their ratings.

CREATING NORMS

Norms are a widely used feedback strategy with 360-degree ratings, although their relevance is sometimes questioned. Norms are usually based on the average ratings on the scales of the 360-degree feedback instrument for a group of individuals who are similar (usually in organizational level) to the feedback recipient. By using the norms, the recipient can compare his or her ratings to those of the group. Such comparisons help the recipient answer the question, How good are my scores relative to the scores of others similar to myself?

For the comparison to be useful and accurate, it is important that the norm group be appropriate for the participant. Comparing the scores of middle managers to a norm base of senior managers, for example, may cause the middle managers to draw negative conclusions about their competence that are not appropriate. Thus, it is important to know whether the norms used for comparison are appropriate for your target group.

Comparisons to norms can take two forms: standard scores and percentile rankings. A standard score is a statistical computation that allows individual scores to be compared to a distribution of scores based on the mean and standard deviation of the total sample. A percentile ranking represents the percentage of persons who have lower scores than the individual being ranked.

CCL believes that appropriate norms are important to help participants understand how their scores compare to the scores of others who are similar to them. This comparison helps them understand whether the competency under consideration is a strength or a development need and helps them identify competencies that they should be focusing on for development.

AGREEMENT BETWEEN SELF-RATINGS AND THE RATINGS OF OTHERS

A continuing controversy is the extent to which self-other agreement (or lack of agreement) is related to performance on the job. It has been thought that individuals whose self-ratings are in agreement with the ratings of others are more effective as leaders, because they have greater self-awareness than those whose self-ratings are not in agreement (Van Velsor, Taylor, & Leslie, 1993). The relationship between self-ratings, others' ratings, and leadership effectiveness, however, appears to be somewhat more complex than previously thought (Atwater, Ostroff, Yammarino, & Fleenor, 1998). Resolving this debate requires more research (for example, Atkins & Wood, 2002).

Atwater, Brett, and Charles (2007) found that, for participants receiving low ratings from others, those who over-rated themselves were more motivated to change their behavior than participants who gave themselves low ratings. The over-raters, however, were found to have more negative reactions to the feedback than those who did not over-rate themselves.

Luthans and Peterson (2003) found that a coaching session that analyzed self-other rating agreement encouraged participants to analyze discrepancies and set goals based on what they learned about themselves. Those who received coaching saw significant improvements in job satisfaction and commitment, as well as in the attitudes of their direct reports.

THE FUTURE OF 360-DEGREE FEEDBACK

Several trends give some indication of the future of 360-degree feedback. These trends include

- A move from centralized scoring services to web-based assessment
- A move from standardized, off-the-shelf instruments to assessments that are customized online for specific organizations
- A move from using 360-degree feedback only with upper- and middle-level management to use with all levels of employees
- A move from presenting only quantitative assessment data to also including written comments
- A belief that 360 feedback can do more than develop leaders and that it can have a positive trickle-down effect on the entire organization

IMPLICATIONS AND APPLICATIONS

This book has presented CCL's perspective on how to best implement the 360-degree feedback process. We hope the recommendations in the book will assist practitioners in organizations in understanding and implementing 360-degree feedback.

In this book, we stress the need for organizations to consider how their business goals align with their goals for implementing 360 feedback. The climate of the organization is critical to the success of 360 feedback. For example, how well does the organization facilitate the feedback process and encourage developmental planning following the feedback? We suggest that professional feedback coaches be used to accomplish these goals.

While research has enlightened the 360 feedback process, many questions remain regarding its implementation. Additional research is needed to fully understand how 360-degree feedback works. For example, what is the best way to ensure that participants will carry out their development plans back on the job? And what is the best method for encouraging raters (peers, direct reports) to fully participate in the process? While these issues are being researched, we encourage practitioners to apply the recommendations in this book to improve the 360-degree feedback process and increase the effectiveness of employees in their organizations.

Sample Presentation for Orientation Session

People at any level of your organization can benefit from 360-degree feedback. New employees need feedback on which skills are important to their jobs, mid-level employees require feedback on their strengths and developmental areas. As employees move up the organizational ladder, they require more feedback on their ability to create a vision for the organization's success.

Be sure to provide the participants with some type of orientation to the 360-degree feedback process. A sample presentation for an orientation session is illustrated in the following pages of this appendix.

360-Degree Feedback

Helping Leaders Become
More Effective

Three Important Lessons

- People can learn, grow, and change.
- Self-awareness is the cornerstone of development.
- Development is an ongoing process intricately related to work.

Role of 360-Degree Feedback

- Allows leaders to see how they are viewed by others
- Highlights strengths and development needs
- Provides a stimulus for change

The Results of 360-Degree Feedback

- Enhanced self-awareness and alignment
- "Unfreezing" behaviors
- Motivation to change

Why Is 360-Degree Feedback Effective for Managers?

- Leadership is relationship intensive.
- Leaders do not naturally get this kind of feedback.
- When the feedback is consistent, it's hard to deny.
- As organizations change, feedback becomes more important.

Copyright © 2007 Center for Creative Leadership

The Development Process Requires...

- Good data from multiple perspectives
  - Reliability
  - Validity
  - Anonymity
  - Confidentiality

Copyright © 2007 Center for Creative Leadership

The Development Process Requires...

- Encouraging openness to feedback
  - Be clear about the purpose.
  - Let participants choose raters.
  - Ensure confidentiality.
  - Provide time to digest the information.
  - Allow for one-to-one work with a feedback coach.
- Appropriate timing for leader's readiness to receive feedback
  - Transitions, "ruts," derailment

The Development Process Requires...

- A development plan
  - Improvement goals
  - Learning strategies
    - Experience (challenges that teach)
    - Ongoing feedback
    - Role models and coaches
    - Training, coursework, and reading
- Organizational support
  - The most direct support comes from the boss.

The Development Process

- An organization has a development orientation if
  - Senior managers participate.
  - Success planning is taken seriously.
  - Bosses are held accountable.
  - All employees have development tasks.
  - Mistakes are treated as learning opportunities.

Leadership Assessment: Issues for Consideration

- Define the business need.
- Look at the organizational culture.
- Review competencies.
- Ensure reliability and validity.
- Examine the research base and expertise.

360-Degree Feedback: Issues for Consideration

Business Need	Organizational Culture	Competencies	Reliability and Validity	Research Base, Expertise
Define	*Ask*	*Review*	*Essential*	*Examine*
• Why am I doing this? • What type of behavior change do I want to encourage? • What are the expected outcomes? • Who is the target population?	• What is the intended **purpose** of the intervention? - Developmental - Evaluative • How does the process **fit** in the organizational context? Is there trust and openness? • Does the process have **integrity**? - Anonymity - Confidentiality - Ownership of data	• Do the items and factors make sense to you? (face validity) • Are the dimensions relevant to the change process? • Do you currently have an underlying management model? • How do the dimensions compare to your model?	• Is the data meaningful to the manager? - Consistent? - Accurate? • Does the instrument assess what it claims to? • Are scores related to effectiveness as a manager, leader, etc.? • Are the behaviors assessed amenable to change?	• What was the process used to develop the instrument? - Theory-based? - Experience-based? - Research-based? • How much experience and expertise does the supplier have with the instrument, target audience, and subject matter?

Copyright © 2007 Center for Creative Leadership

Why Use Assessment Instruments?

- Comparison of intentions to perceptions
- Multiple perceptions
- Baseline information, self-awareness
- Perceived impact of behavior
- Key driver of development

Copyright © 2007 Center for Creative Leadership

Appendix A: Sample Presentation for Orientation Session   **77**

Development versus Performance

- CCL believes the major goal of feedback is individual development.

- Feedback used for input into performance appraisals has a different purpose and should be kept separate.

Assessment Instruments: CCL Philosophy and Usage

- They should support and encourage learning and growth.
- Self-awareness is the cornerstone of development.
- They should be research-based, reliable, and valid.
- There is a commitment to confidentiality.
- Feedback and development of planning are critical to the process.

360-Degree Feedback Used for Developmental Purposes

- Increased honesty from raters
- Psychological safety and ethical standards
- Ownership of data–individual accountability
- Commitment to change behavior–credible process
- Adult learning–change comes from within
- New understanding and broader capacity

Glossary of 360-Degree Feedback Terms

360-degree feedback. A process in which feedback information is obtained from more than one source. The information is usually related to a person's job-related behavior. Sources can include the individual and his or her manager, coworkers, direct reports, customers (internal or external), and anyone else who is in a position to provide job-related feedback.

anonymity. Anonymity means that no one will be able to identify which data was provided by any individual rater. It protects raters against retaliation for providing negative feedback and serves as a safeguard to ensure that the ratings gathered are candid and accurate. Anonymity is usually ensured by averaging the individual ratings within particular rater groups (direct reports, peers, and so on) and by not reporting the ratings for a group unless the number of raters exceeds a minimum (usually three).

coach. A consultant (internal or external) who specializes in 360-degree feedback, sometimes also called a facilitator. A coach delivers feedback and helps participants identify their development needs and prepare their development plans.

competency. A characteristic or attribute of an individual that is related to effective performance in a job or leadership role. In the case of leadership development, it's typically an individual's knowledge, skills, abilities, personality, and other characteristics.

competency scale training. A type of rater training that prepares raters by exposing them to the scales and items before they provide responses, which can increase rater accuracy.

confidentiality. An important aspect of developmental 360-degree feedback processes whereby only the participants and their coaches have access to the feedback report. Participants may share the results with their bosses and/or staffs, a practice that is encouraged by some feedback professionals. However, it is the participant's decision whether or not to share this information.

development need. A gap between how a person is currently performing and how the person should be performing. A development need can arise from a failure to achieve a goal or from the realization that a competency has to be more fully developed.

development plan. A plan for addressing development needs, such as becoming more effective in a current job, making better use of an underused strength, or preparing to take on greater responsibilities. It focuses on changing behavior to achieve goals.

feedback. Information that addresses a person's behavior and the results of that behavior. Feedback is usually intended to reinforce desired behaviors or to suggest changes in undesired behaviors, and it can be a powerful stimulus for change.

frame-of-reference training. A type of rater training that involves calibrating each scale by using a list of behaviors that correspond to performance levels in the organization (that is, what constitutes effective and ineffective behaviors in that organization).

goal. A desired outcome that a person strives to achieve.

halo errors. Errors made by raters when they generalize their ratings across the items on the instrument—for example, rating a participant high on all items because he or she is outstanding on one particular item.

instrument. Any kind of tool or device that is used to collect information in a structured, systematic way. Examples of instruments include tests, performance evaluation forms, surveys, and questionnaires.

instrument reactivity. The way an instrument "reacts" when it is administered to the same participants a second time. Because both the participants and raters have experienced the process before, they may respond differently than they did the first time. For example, raters may expect that the participants will have improved their leadership effectiveness as a result of having gone through the development process previously.

norms. A method for comparing a participant's results with the average ratings from a relevant comparison group. In 360-degree feedback, feedback reports can present norms alongside results so that participants can see how they stack up against others in similar jobs.

off-the-shelf. A generic version of an instrument that is purchased from the supplier without customization.

participant. The person who receives the feedback in a 360-degree process. The participant uses the feedback to identify areas for improvement and areas representing strengths.

psychometrics. The quantitative science of measuring the quality (reliability and validity, for example) of data gathered by 360-degree feedback and other instruments.

rater. A respondent who provides feedback. The rater should be someone who has worked with the participant during the past year and who can provide appropriate and relevant feedback.

rating scale. A structured way for responding to items on an instrument. Most rating scales provide the rater with a numeric scale on which each point of the scale is anchored by a descriptive term.

recency errors. Errors made by raters when they base their ratings only on their most recent experiences with the participant, rather than on a longer, more appropriate, period of time.

reliability. Consistency, or accuracy. There are three aspects to reliability: internal consistency within scales, agreement within rater groups, and stability of the ratings over time.

SBI (situation-behavior-impact). A simple feedback method that keeps comments relevant and focused to increase their effectiveness. With SBI, the situation in which the behavior was observed and the impact of that behavior are described.

scale. Related items that are grouped together to represent a competency on a feedback report. Items on the same scale have logical and empirical consistency. Usually, the ratings of the items on a scale are averaged to calculate a score for the competency measured by that scale.

temporal validity. The effects of organizational changes on 360 ratings when an instrument is used for a second time in the same organization. As a result of these changes, raters may respond differently on the second administration.

validity. The extent to which an instrument measures what it is intended to measure; the appropriateness of the ways scores from an instrument are used.

verbatim bias. The tendency for participants to give more attention to written comments in their feedback reports than to numerical or graphical scores.

REFERENCES

Antonioni, D. (1994). The effects of feedback accountability on upward appraisal ratings. *Personnel Psychology, 47,* 349–356.

Atkins, P. W. B., & Wood, R. E. (2002). Self- versus others' ratings as predictors of assessment center ratings: Validation evidence for 360-degree feedback programs. *Personnel Psychology, 55,* 871–904.

Atwater, L. E., Brett, J. F., & Charles, A. C. (2007). Multisource feedback: Lessons learned and implications for practice. *Human Resource Management, 46,* 285–307.

Atwater, L. E., Ostroff, C., Yammarino, F., & Fleenor, J. W. (1998). Self-other agreement: Does it matter? *Personnel Psychology, 51,* 577–598.

Atwater, L. E., & Waldman, D. A. (1998, May). Accountability in 360-degree feedback. *HRMagazine, 43,* 96–104.

Atwater, L., Waldman, D., Atwater, D., & Cartier, T. (2000). An upward feedback field experiment. Supervisors' cynicism, follow-up, and commitment to subordinates. *Personnel Psychology, 53,* 275–297.

Berke, D., Kossler, M. E., & Wakefield, M. (2008). *Developing leadership talent.* San Francisco: Pfeiffer.

Bracken, D. W. (1996). Multisource (360-degree) feedback: Surveys for individual and organizational development. In A. I. Kraut (Ed.), *Organizational surveys: Tools for assessment and change* (pp. 117–143). San Francisco: Jossey-Bass.

Bracken, D. W., Dalton, M. A., Jako, R. A., McCauley, C. D., & Pollman, V. A. (1997). *Should 360-degree feedback be used only for developmental purposes?* Greensboro, NC: Center for Creative Leadership.

Bracken, D. W., Summers, L., & Fleenor, J. W. (1998). High-tech 360. *Training and Development, 52*(8), 42–45.

Bracken, D. W., Timmreck, C., & Church, A. (Eds.) (2001). *The handbook of multisource feedback.* San Francisco: Jossey-Bass.

Bracken, D. W., Timmreck, C., Fleenor, J. W., & Summers, L. (2001). 360 feedback from another angle. *Human Resource Management, 40,* 3–20.

Bradley, J. (2001). *Value positioning tracker study 2001: Industry and client analysis.* Greensboro, NC: Center for Creative Leadership.

Brett, J. F., & Atwater, L. E. (2001). 360-degree feedback: Accuracy, reactions, and perceptions of usefulness. *Journal of Applied Psychology, 86,* 930–942.

Brutus, S., & Derayeh, M. (2002). Multisource assessment programs in organizations: An insider's perspective. *Human Resource Development Quarterly, 13,* 187–202.

Brutus, S., Fleenor, J. W., & London, M. (1998). Elements of effective 360-degree feedback. In W. W. Tornow & M. London (Eds.), *Maximizing the value of 360-degree feedback: A process for successful individual and organizational development* (pp. 11–27). San Francisco: Jossey-Bass.

Chappelow, C. T. (2004). 360-degree feedback. In C. D. McCauley & E. Van Velsor (Eds.), *The Center for Creative Leadership handbook of leadership development* (2nd ed., pp. 58–84). San Francisco: Jossey-Bass.

Church, A. H. (2000). Do higher performing managers actually receive better ratings? A validation of multirater assessment methodology. *Consulting Psychology Journal: Practice and Research, 52,* 99–116.

Dalessio, A. (1998). Using multisource feedback for employee development and personnel decisions. In J. W. Smither (Ed.), *Performance appraisal: State of the art in practice* (pp. 278–330). San Francisco: Jossey-Bass.

Dalton, M. A. (1998). Best practices: Five rationales for using 360-degree feedback in organizations. In W. W. Tornow & M. London (Eds.), *Maximizing the value of 360-degree feedback: A process for successful individual and organizational development* (pp. 59–77). San Francisco: Jossey-Bass.

Fleenor, J. W., & Brutus, S. (2001). Multisource feedback for personnel decisions. In D. W. Bracken, C. Timmreck, & A. Church (Eds.), *The handbook of multisource feedback* (pp. 335–351). San Francisco: Jossey-Bass.

Goldsmith, M., & Underhill, B. (2001). Multisource feedback for executive development. In D. W. Bracken, C. Timmreck, & A. Church (Eds.), *The handbook of multisource feedback* (pp. 275–288). San Francisco: Jossey-Bass.

Hannum, K., & Martineau, J. (2008). *Evaluating the impact of leadership development.* San Francisco: Pfeiffer.

Hazucha, J., Hezlett, S., & Schneider, R. J. (1993). The impact of 360-degree feedback on management skills development. *Human Resource Management, 32,* 325–351.

Healy, M. C., Walsh, A. B., & Rose, D. S. (2003). *A benchmarking study of North American 360-degree feedback practices.* Presented at the 18th annual convention of the Society for Industrial and Organizational Psychology, Orlando, Florida.

Hedge, J., Borman, W., & Berkland, S. (2001). History and development of multisource feedback as a methodology. In D. W. Bracken, C. Timmreck, & A. Church (Eds.), *The handbook of multisource feedback* (pp. 15–32). San Francisco: Jossey-Bass.

Kaplan, R. E., Drath, W. H., & Kofodimos, J. R. (1985). *High hurdles: The challenge of executive self-development* (Technical Report No. 125). Greensboro, NC: Center for Creative Leadership.

Kirkpatrick, D. L. (1975). *Evaluating training programs.* Madison, WI: ASTD.

Kozlowski, S., Chao, G., & Morrison, R. (1998). Games raters play: Politics, strategies, and impression management in performance appraisal. In J. W. Smither (Ed.), *Performance appraisal: State of the art in practice* (pp. 163–205). San Francisco: Jossey-Bass.

Lepsinger, R., & Lucia, A. (1997). *The art and science of 360-degree feedback.* San Francisco: Pfeiffer.

Leslie, J. B., & Fleenor, J. W. (1998). *Feedback to managers: A review and comparison of multi-rater instruments for management development* (3rd ed.). Greensboro, NC: Center for Creative Leadership.

London, M. (1997). *Job feedback: Giving, seeking and using feedback for performance improvement.* Mahwah, NJ: Lawrence Erlbaum Associates.

London, M. (2001). The great debate: Should multisource feedback be used for administration or development only? In D. W. Bracken, C. Timmreck, & A. Church (Eds.), *The handbook of multisource feedback* (pp. 368–387). San Francisco: Jossey-Bass.

London, M., & Beatty, R. W. (1993). 360-degree feedback as a competitive advantage. *Human Resource Management, 32,* 353–372.

London, M., & Smither, J. W. (1995). Can multi-source feedback change self-evaluation, skill development, and performance? *Personnel Psychology, 48,* 375–390.

Luthans, F., & Peterson, S. J. (2003). 360-degree feedback with systematic coaching: Empirical analysis suggests a winning combination. *Human Resource Management, 42,* 243–256.

Maurer, T. J., Mitchell, D., & Barbeite, F. G. (2002). Predictors of attitudes toward a 360-degree feedback system and involvement in post-feedback management development activity. *Journal of Occupational and Organizational Psychology, 75,* 87–107.

McCall, M. W., Lombardo, M. M., & Morrison, A. M. (1988). *The lessons of experience: How successful executives develop on the job.* Lexington, MA: Lexington Books.

McCauley, C. D., & Moxley, R. (1996). Developmental 360: How feedback can make managers more effective. *Career Development International, 1*(3), 15–19.

Morrison, A. M., McCall, M. W., & DeVries, D. L. (1978). *Feedback to managers: A comprehensive review of twenty-four instruments.* Greensboro, NC: Center for Creative Leadership.

Seifert, C. F., Yukl, G., & McDonald, R. A. (2003). Effects of multisource feedback and a feedback facilitator on the influence behavior of managers towards subordinates. *Journal of Applied Psychology, 88,* 561–569.

Smither, J. W., London, M., Flautt, R., Vargas, Y., & Kucine, I. (2003). Can executive coaches enhance the impact of multi-source feedback on behavior change? A quasi-experimental field study. *Personnel Psychology, 56,* 23–44.

Smither, J. W., London, M., & Reilly, R. R. (2005). Does performance improve following multi-source feedback? A theoretical model, meta-analysis, and review of empirical findings. *Personnel Psychology, 58*, 33–66.

Smither, J. W., London, M., Reilly, R. R., Flautt, R., Vargas, Y., & Kucine, T. (2004). Discussing multisource feedback with raters and performance improvement. *Journal of Management Development, 23*, 456–468.

Testa, M. R. (2002). A model for organizational-based 360 degree leadership assessment. *Leadership & Organization Development Journal, 23*, 260–269.

Timmreck, C., & Bracken, D. W. (1995, May). *Upward feedback in the trenches: Challenges and realities.* Paper presented at the meeting of the Society for Industrial and Organizational Psychology, Orlando, Florida.

Timmreck, C., & Bracken, D. W. (1997). Multisource feedback: A study of its use in decision making. *Employee Relations, 24*, 21–27.

Tornow, W. W. (Ed.). (1993). 360-degree feedback [Special issue]. *Human Resource Management, 32* (2, 3).

Tornow, W. W., London, M., & CCL Associates. (1998). *Maximizing the value of 360-degree feedback: A process for successful individual and organizational development.* San Francisco: Jossey-Bass.

Van Velsor, E. (1998). Designing 360-degree feedback to enhance involvement, self-determination, and commitment. In W. W. Tornow & M. London (Eds.), *Maximizing the value of 360-degree feedback: A process for successful individual and organizational development* (pp. 149–195). San Francisco: Jossey-Bass.

Van Velsor, E., & Leslie, J. B. (1991). *Feedback to managers, volume II: A review and comparison of sixteen multi-rater feedback instruments.* Greensboro, NC: Center for Creative Leadership.

Van Velsor, E., Leslie, J. B., & Fleenor, J. W. (1997). *Choosing 360: A guide to evaluating multi-rater feedback instruments for management development.* Greensboro, NC: Center for Creative Leadership.

Van Velsor, E., Taylor, S., & Leslie, J. B. (1993). An examination of the relationships among self-perception accuracy, self-awareness, gender, and leader effectiveness. *Human Resource Management, 32*, 249–264.

Waldman, D. A., & Atwater, L. E. (1998). *The power of 360-degree feedback: How to leverage performance evaluations for top productivity.* Houston, TX: Gulf.

Waldman, D. A., Atwater, L. E., & Antonioni, D. (1998). Has 360 degree feedback gone amok? *The Academy of Management Executive, 12*, 86–94.

Walker, A. G., & Smither, J. W. (1999). A five-year study of upward feedback: What managers do with their results matters. *Personnel Psychology, 52*, 393–423.

RECOMMENDED RESOURCES

Antonioni, D. (1996). Designing an effective 360-degree appraisal feedback process. *Organizational Dynamics, 25*, 24–38.

Atwater, L., & Brett, J. (in press). Feedback format: Does it influence managers' reactions to feedback. *Journal of Occupational and Organizational Psychology.*

Atwater, L., & Brett, J. (2005). Antecedents and consequences of reactions to developmental 360-degree feedback. *Journal of Vocational Behavior, 66*, 532–548.

Atwater, L., & Brett, J. (2006). 360-degree feedback to leaders: Does it relate to changes in employee attitudes? *Group & Organization Management, 31*, 578–600.

Atwater, L., Roush, P., & Fischthal, A. (1995). The influence of upward feedback on self- and follower ratings of leadership. *Personnel Psychology, 48*, 35–59.

Bailey, C., & Fletcher, C. (2002). The impact of multiple source feedback on management development: Findings from a longitudinal study. *Journal of Organizational Behavior, 23*, 853–867.

Beehr, T. A., Ivanitskaya, L., Hansen, C., Erofeev, D., & Gudanowski, D. (2001). Evaluation of 360-degree feedback ratings: Relationships with each other and with performance and selection predictors. *Journal of Organizational Behavior, 22*, 775–788.

Bracken, D. W. (1994). Straight talk about multirater feedback. *Training and Development, 48*(9), 44–51.

Brutus, S., Fleenor, J. W., & McCauley, C. D. (1999). Demographic and personality predictors of congruence in multi-source ratings. *Journal of Management Development, 18*, 417–435.

Brutus, S., Fleenor, J. W., & Tisak, J. (1999). Exploring the link between rating congruence and managerial effectiveness. *Canadian Journal of Administrative Sciences, 16*, 308–322.

Campbell, D. (2001). Foreword. In D. W. Bracken, C. Timmreck, & A. Church (Eds.), *The handbook of multisource feedback* (pp. xii–xx). San Francisco: Jossey-Bass.

Dalton, M. A. (1996). Multirater feedback and conditions for change. *Consulting Psychology Journal, 48*, 12–16.

DeNisi, A., & Kluger, A. (2000). Feedback effectiveness: Can 360-degree appraisals be improved? *The Academy of Management Executive, 14*, 129–139.

Edwards, M., & Ewen, A. (1996). *360-degree feedback: The powerful new model for employee assessment and performance improvement.* New York: AMACOM.

Edwards, M., & Ewen, A. (1998, May). *Multisource assessment survey of industry practice, 1998.* Paper presented at the 360-Degree Feedback Global Users Conference, Orlando, Florida.

Fleenor, J. W., McCauley, C. D., & Brutus, S. (1996). Self-other rating agreement and leader effectiveness. *Leadership Quarterly, 7*, 487–506.

Fleenor, J. W., & Prince, J. M. (1997). *Using 360-degree feedback in organizations: An annotated bibliography.* Greensboro, NC: Center for Creative Leadership.

Gruner, S. (1997, February). Feedback from everyone. *Inc., 19*, 102–103.

Haward, S. (1998, May). The dark side of multi-rater assessments. *HRMagazine, 43*, 106–114.

Hegarty, W. H. (1974). Using subordinate ratings to elicit behavioral changes in supervisors. *Journal of Applied Psychology, 59*, 764–766.

Heslin, P., & Latham, G. (2004). The effect of upward feedback on managerial behavior. *Applied Psychology: An International Review, 53*, 23–37.

Hirsch, M. (1994, August). 360 degrees of evaluation. *Working Woman, 19*, 20–21.

Hoffman, R. (1995, April). Ten reasons you should be using 360-degree feedback. *HRMagazine, 40*, 82–85.

Howard, A., Byham, W., & Hauenstein, P. (1994). *Multirater assessment and feedback: Applications, implementation, and implications.* Pittsburgh, PA: DDI.

Johnson, J. W., & Ferstl, K. L. (1999). The effects of interrater and self-other agreement on performance improvement following upward feedback. *Personnel Psychology, 52*, 271–303.

Jones, J. E., & Bearley, W. (1996). *360-degree feedback: Strategies, tactics, and techniques for developing leaders.* Amherst, MA: HRD Press.

Jude-York, D., & Wise, S. (1997). *Multipoint feedback: A 360-degree catalyst for change.* Menlo Park, CA: Crisp.

Lassiter, D. (1996, May/June). A user's guide to 360 feedback. *Performance and Instruction, 35*, 12–15.

Lepsinger, R., & Lucia, A. (1997). 360-degree feedback and performance appraisal. *Training, 34*(9), 62–70.

Levy, P. W., & Williams, J. R. (2004). The social context of performance appraisal: A review and framework for the future. *Journal of Management, 30*, 881–905.

Lindsey, E., Homes, V., & McCall, M. W., Jr. (1987). *Key events in executives' lives.* Greensboro, NC: Center for Creative Leadership.

London, M. (2003). *Job feedback.* Mahwah, NJ: Lawrence Erlbaum Associates.

Mabey, C. (2001). Closing the circle: Participant views of a 360 degree feedback programme. *Human Resource Management Journal, 11*, 41–54.

Nowack, K. (1993). 360-degree feedback: The whole story. *Training and Development,* *47*(1), 69–72.

Nowack, K. M. (1992). Self-assessment and rater-assessment as a dimension of management development. *Human Resource Development Quarterly, 3,* 141–155.

Reilly, R. R., Smither, J. W., & Vasilopoulos, N. L. (1996). A longitudinal study of upward feedback. *Personnel Psychology, 49,* 599–612.

Ryan, A., Brutus, S., Greguras, G., & Hakel, M. (2000). Receptivity to assessment-based feedback for management development. *Journal of Management Development, 19,* 252–276.

Smither, J. W. (Ed.). (1998). *Performance appraisal: State of the art in practice.* San Francisco: Jossey-Bass.

Smither, J. W., London, M., & Richmond, K. R. (2005). The relationship between leaders' personality and their reactions to and use of multisource feedback: A longitudinal study. *Group & Organization Management, 30,* 181–211.

Smither, J. W., London, M., Vasilopoulos, N. L., Reilly, R. R., Millsap, R. E., & Salvemini, N. (1995). An examination of the effects of an upward feedback program over time. *Personnel Psychology, 48,* 1–34.

Smither, J. W., Walker, A. G., & Yap, M. (2004). An examination of the equivalence of web-based versus paper-and-pencil upward feedback ratings: Rater- and ratee-level analyses. *Education and Psychological Measurement, 64,* 40–61.

Summers, L., & Fleenor, J. W. (1998). Information technology spurs the evolution of 360-degree feedback. *Leadership in Action, 10*(4), 9–13.

Tornow, W. W. (Ed.). (1993). 360-degree feedback [Special issue]. *Human Resource Management, 32*(2, 3).

Tornow, W. W. (1998). Forces that affect the 360-degree feedback process. In W. W. Tornow & M. London (Eds.), *Maximizing the value of 360-degree feedback: A process for successful individual and organizational development* (pp. 78–100). San Francisco: Jossey-Bass.

Van Velsor, E., & Fleenor, J. W. (1997). The MBTI and leadership skills: A comparison of its relationship to five 360-degree instruments. In C. Fitzgerald & L. K. Kirby (Eds.), *Developing leaders: Research and applications in psychological type and leadership development* (pp. 139–162). Palo Alto, CA: Davies-Black.

Ward, P. (1997). *360-degree feedback.* London: Institute of Personnel Development.

Wimer, S., & Nowack, K. (1998). 13 common mistakes using 360-degree feedback. *Training and Development, 52*(5), 69–80.

Yukl, G., & Lepsinger, R. (1995). How to get the most out of 360-degree feedback. *Training, 32*(12), 45–50.

INDEX

ABOUT THE AUTHORS

John Fleenor is the group director of Knowledge and Innovation Resources (KIR) at the Center for Creative Leadership (CCL). Additionally, John conducts research in areas such as instrument development and quantitative methods. As leader of feedback research at the Center, he has been responsible for research on the development and use of 360-degree feedback instruments.

John is a coauthor of three CCL publications: *Feedback to Managers: A Review and Comparison of Multi-Rater Instruments for Management Development; Using 360-Degree Feedback in Organizations: An Annotated Bibliography;* and *Choosing 360: A Guide to Evaluating Multi-Rater Feedback Instruments for Management Development.* He has also published several book chapters and numerous journal articles on 360-degree feedback and related topics.

John holds a Ph.D. in industrial/organizational psychology from North Carolina State University. He is an adjunct member of the psychology faculties at NCSU and at the University of North Carolina at Charlotte. John has taught graduate-level organizational psychology courses, and serves on the dissertation committees of several psychology graduate students. John serves on the editorial board of *Human Resource Management Journal,* and he is a member of the American Psychological Association and the Society for Industrial and Organizational Psychology.

Sylvester Taylor is director, Global Assessment and Development Resources, at CCL. His group is responsible for development, management, and distribution of CCL's assessment instruments, as well as other products that support learning and development. These include 360 BY DESIGN, Benchmarks, EdgeWork,

Executive Dimensions, KEYS, LEAD, Prospector, and SKILLSCOPE. Sylvester has partnered with CCL clients to design and implement strategic 360-degree feedback initiatives for all levels of management. In addition to certifying professionals on the use of CCL 360s, he facilitates feedback to groups and individuals at the highest leadership levels.

Prior to joining CCL, Sylvester worked as an administrator and as an instructor at the University of North Carolina in Chapel Hill, North Carolina, teaching courses in psychology and statistics. He has published and edited numerous articles in scholarly and professional journals related to creativity, leadership development, psychological measurement, and organizational effectiveness. Sylvester holds a B.S. degree in economics and industrial relations from the University of North Carolina at Chapel Hill, and he has completed extensive graduate course work in psychometrics, psychology, and adult education.

Craig Chappelow is a senior manager at CCL, where he divides his time between working with clients and managing Executive Dimensions, CCL's 360-degree assessment instrument developed exclusively for use with the top-level leaders in an organization. His areas of specialization include the interpretation and delivery of instrument-based feedback to senior executives and the development of effective senior executive teams. As a member of the CCL faculty, he is a senior trainer in a number of CCL's open-enrollment and custom programs.

In addition to the United States, Craig has worked with executives in China, Belgium, Canada, Australia, New Zealand, Bermuda, France, Dubai, Luxembourg, and the United Kingdom. He is author of a book chapter entitled "360-Degree Feedback," which appears in *The Center for Creative Leadership Handbook of Leadership Development* (Jossey-Bass, 2004), and coauthor of *Keeping Your Career on Track*, a guidebook for managers published by CCL. He also has published articles in a wide variety of sources, including *Harvard Business Review*.

Craig was originally trained as a chemist, and his work experience includes technical positions at Glidden Corporation and National Starch and Chemical Company. Craig holds a bachelor's degree from MacMurray College and a master's degree from the University of Vermont.

Pfeiffer Publications Guide

This guide is designed to familiarize you with the various types of Pfeiffer publications. The formats section describes the various types of products that we publish; the methodologies section describes the many different ways that content might be provided within a product. We also provide a list of the topic areas in which we publish.

FORMATS

In addition to its extensive book-publishing program, Pfeiffer offers content in an array of formats, from fieldbooks for the practitioner to complete, ready-to-use training packages that support group learning.

FIELDBOOK Designed to provide information and guidance to practitioners in the midst of action. Most fieldbooks are companions to another, sometimes earlier, work, from which its ideas are derived; the fieldbook makes practical what was theoretical in the original text. Fieldbooks can certainly be read from cover to cover. More likely, though, you'll find yourself bouncing around following a particular theme, or dipping in as the mood, and the situation, dictate.

HANDBOOK A contributed volume of work on a single topic, comprising an eclectic mix of ideas, case studies, and best practices sourced by practitioners and experts in the field.

An editor or team of editors usually is appointed to seek out contributors and to evaluate content for relevance to the topic. Think of a handbook not as a ready-to-eat meal, but as a cookbook of ingredients that enables you to create the most fitting experience for the occasion.

RESOURCE Materials designed to support group learning. They come in many forms: a complete, ready-to-use exercise (such as a game); a comprehensive resource on one topic (such as conflict management) containing a variety of methods and approaches; or a collection of like-minded activities (such as icebreakers) on multiple subjects and situations.

TRAINING PACKAGE An entire, ready-to-use learning program that focuses on a particular topic or skill. All packages comprise a guide for the facilitator/trainer and a workbook for the participants. Some packages are supported with additional media—such as video—or learning aids, instruments, or other devices to help participants understand concepts or practice and develop skills.

- *Facilitator/trainer's guide* Contains an introduction to the program, advice on how to organize and facilitate the learning event, and step-by-step instructor notes. The guide also contains copies of presentation materials—handouts, presentations, and overhead designs, for example—used in the program.

- *Participant's workbook* Contains exercises and reading materials that support the learning goal and serves as a valuable reference and support guide for participants in the weeks and months that follow the learning event. Typically, each participant will require his or her own workbook.

ELECTRONIC CD-ROMs and web-based products transform static Pfeiffer content into dynamic, interactive experiences. Designed to take advantage of the searchability, automation, and ease-of-use that technology provides, our e-products bring convenience and immediate accessibility to your workspace.

METHODOLOGIES

CASE STUDY A presentation, in narrative form, of an actual event that has occurred inside an organization. Case studies are not prescriptive, nor are they used to prove a point; they are designed to develop critical analysis and decision-making skills. A case study has a specific time frame, specifies a sequence of events, is narrative in structure, and contains a plot structure—an issue (what should be/have been done?). Use case studies when the goal is to enable participants to apply previously learned theories to the circumstances in the case, decide what is pertinent, identify the real issues, decide what should have been done, and develop a plan of action.

ENERGIZER A short activity that develops readiness for the next session or learning event. Energizers are most commonly used after a break or lunch to stimulate or refocus the group. Many involve some form of physical activity, so they are a useful way to counter post-lunch lethargy. Other uses include transitioning from one topic to another, where "mental" distancing is important.

EXPERIENTIAL LEARNING ACTIVITY (ELA) A facilitator-led intervention that moves participants through the learning cycle from experience to application (also known as a Structured Experience). ELAs are carefully thought-out designs in which there is a definite learning purpose and intended outcome. Each step—everything that participants do during the activity—facilitates the accomplishment of the stated goal. Each ELA includes complete instructions for facilitating the intervention and a clear statement of goals, suggested group size and timing, materials required, an explanation of the process, and, where appropriate, possible variations to the activity. (For more detail on Experiential

Learning Activities, see the Introduction to the *Reference Guide to Handbooks and Annuals*, 1999 edition, Pfeiffer, San Francisco.)

GAME   A group activity that has the purpose of fostering team spirit and togetherness in addition to the achievement of a pre-stated goal. Usually contrived—undertaking a desert expedition, for example—this type of learning method offers an engaging means for participants to demonstrate and practice business and interpersonal skills. Games are effective for team building and personal development mainly because the goal is subordinate to the process—the means through which participants reach decisions, collaborate, communicate, and generate trust and understanding. Games often engage teams in "friendly" competition.

ICEBREAKER   A (usually) short activity designed to help participants overcome initial anxiety in a training session and/or to acquaint the participants with one another. An icebreaker can be a fun activity or can be tied to specific topics or training goals. While a useful tool in itself, the icebreaker comes into its own in situations where tension or resistance exists within a group.

INSTRUMENT A device used to assess, appraise, evaluate, describe, classify, and summarize various aspects of human behavior. The term used to describe an instrument depends primarily on its format and purpose. These terms include survey, questionnaire, inventory, diagnostic, survey, and poll. Some uses of instruments include providing instrumental feedback to group members, studying here-and-now processes or functioning within a group, manipulating group composition, and evaluating outcomes of training and other interventions.

Instruments are popular in the training and HR field because, in general, more growth can occur if an individual is provided with a method for focusing specifically on his or her own behavior. Instruments also are used to obtain information that will serve as a basis for change and to assist in workforce planning efforts.

Paper-and-pencil tests still dominate the instrument landscape with a typical package comprising a facilitator's guide, which offers advice on administering the instrument and interpreting the collected data, and an initial set of instruments. Additional instruments are available separately. Pfeiffer, though, is investing heavily in e-instruments. Electronic instrumentation provides effortless distribution and, for larger groups particularly, offers advantages over paper-and-pencil tests in the time it takes to analyze data and provide feedback.

LECTURETTE   A short talk that provides an explanation of a principle, model, or process that is pertinent to the participants' current learning needs. A lecturette is intended to establish a common language bond between the trainer and the participants by providing a mutual frame of reference. Use a lecturette as an introduction to a group activity or event, as an interjection during an event, or as a handout.

MODEL A graphic depiction of a system or process and the relationship among its elements. Models provide a frame of reference and something more tangible, and more easily remembered, than a verbal explanation. They also give participants something to "go on," enabling them to track their own progress as they experience the dynamics, processes, and relationships being depicted in the model.

ROLE PLAY A technique in which people assume a role in a situation/scenario: a customer service rep in an angry-customer exchange, for example. The way in which the role is approached is then discussed and feedback is offered. The role play is often repeated using a different approach and/or incorporating changes made based on feedback received. In other words, role playing is a spontaneous interaction involving realistic behavior under artificial (and safe) conditions.

SIMULATION A methodology for understanding the interrelationships among components of a system or process. Simulations differ from games in that they test or use a model that depicts or mirrors some aspect of reality in form, if not necessarily in content. Learning occurs by studying the effects of change on one or more factors of the model. Simulations are commonly used to test hypotheses about what happens in a system—often referred to as "what if?" analysis—or to examine best-case/worst-case scenarios.

THEORY A presentation of an idea from a conjectural perspective. Theories are useful because they encourage us to examine behavior and phenomena through a different lens.

TOPICS

The twin goals of providing effective and practical solutions for workforce training and organization development and meeting the educational needs of training and human resource professionals shape Pfeiffer's publishing program. Core topics include the following:

Leadership & Management

Communication & Presentation

Coaching & Mentoring

Training & Development

E-Learning

Teams & Collaboration

OD & Strategic Planning

Human Resources

Consulting

What will you find on pfeiffer.com?

- The best in workplace performance solutions for training and HR professionals

- Downloadable training tools, exercises, and content

- Web-exclusive offers

- Training tips, articles, and news

- Seamless on-line ordering

- Author guidelines, information on becoming a Pfeiffer Affiliate, and much more

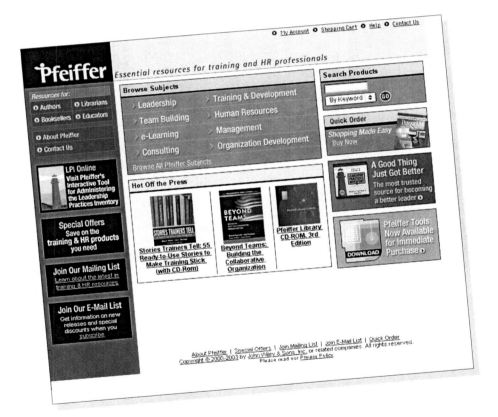

Discover more at www.pfeiffer.com

ADDITIONAL RESOURCES

360-DEGREE ASSESSMENTS

We encourage you to find more ways to implement 360-Degree Assessments in your work. Here are some options from Pfeiffer and CCL.

Pfeiffer

- Leadership Practices Inventory (LPI)/LPIOnline.com
- Diversity Mosaic/The Complete Resource for Establishing a Successful Diversity Initiative
- Global Executive Leadership Inventory/GELIOnline.com

Please visit www.pfeiffer.com to find out more about the above assessments and other Pfeiffer products. If you would like to receive a free sample assessment or online demo, please call one of our assessment consultants toll free at 866-888-5159.

Center for Creative Leadership (CCL)

- Executive Dimensions®—www.ccl.org/execdimensions
- Benchmarks®—www.ccl.org/benchmarks
- Prospector®—www.ccl.org/prospector
- 360 BY DESIGN®—www.ccl.org/360bd
- SKILLSCOPE®—www.ccl.org/skillscope

Please visit www.ccl.org to find out more about CCL's assessments and other products and programs.

CPSIA information can be obtained at www.ICGtesting.com
Printed in the USA
BVOW05n2126061113

335637BV00003B/3/P